MW01222119

English Grammar
Principles and Facts

Second Edition

Jeffrey P. Kaplan

Prentice Hall, Englewood Cliffs, New Jersey 07632

©1995 by PRENTICE-HALL, INC.
A Simon and Schuster Company
Englewood Cliffs, New Jersey 07632

10 9 8 7 6 5 4 3 2 1

ISBN 0-13-356759-1
Printed in the United States of America

ENGLISH GRAMMAR: PRINCIPLES AND FACTS, Second Edition

Answers to Exercises

Chapter One. Some Ways of Thinking About Grammar

Exercise 1: No single right answer.

Exercise 2: No single right answer.

Exercise 3:

1. Loss of *who/whom* distinction: Could be answered either way. *Whom* marked (or marks) objective case (i.e., uses other than as subject or possessive): In *Whom will we see,* the word *whom* functions as direct object, in contrast with *who* in *Who will go,* in which *who* functions as subject. This distinction is grammatical; is it also meaningful? Sure; but this is the kind of meaning that is commonly called "grammatical meaning." One reason to call *whom/'whom* distinction merely grammatical is that no misunderstanding could occur as a result of its loss; object function is always signaled redundantly. In *Whom will we see,* the fact that *whom* functions as object follows from the fact that the transitive verb *see* lacks a direct object in its customary post-verbal position and from the existence of wh- movement placing *whom* in sentence-initial position.

2. *Disinterested* as synonym for *uninterested:* Loss of a meaning distinction. *Disinterested* means 'unbiased, not influenced by self-interest'; *uninterested* means 'not interested, unconcerned.'

3. *They* taking a singular antecedent: merely a grammatical change, with no loss of a meaning distinction.

4. *Not as tall as* instead of *not so tall as:* merely a grammatical change.

5. *I was literally climbing the walls* to mean 'I was distraught': Loss of a meaning distinction; *literally* means 'according to primary meaning, as contrasted with metaphorical or exaggerated meaning.'

6. *Most* for *almost:* Merely a grammatical change.

7. *Between you and I:* Merely a grammatical change. Object function is signaled by the presence of the preposition, so the subjective case form *I* could not possibly be misinterpreted as the grammatical function "subject."

Exercise 4:

Loss of 2d person singular pronouns: unfortunate, beneficial, or harmless? The argument for saying "beneficial": the change has resulted in a simpler, easier-to-learn system, helpful, e.g., for many second-language learners. But a stronger argument is that the loss of these pronouns is unfortunate, since a significant meaning distinction is no longer morphologically marked. English is poorer, one may believe, than most European languages, which have the a distinction (e.g., French *tu* vs. *vous*) which enables speakers efficiently to encode power and solidarity relations.

Exercise 5. Lots of different responses are possible.

1. *This shirt needs ironed:* Pittsburghian.
2. *They might should go:* Southern double modal construction.
3. *...so don't I·* age-graded (age 12 or so) Bostonian. Means '...so do I.'
4. *She always be late:* Black English. Means: habitual, typical.
5. *Don't nobody know that:* Black English.
6. *That is John book.* Black English.
7. *There's a new house abuilding:* Ozarkan.
8. *My brother a firefighter.* Black English.
9. *There goes the man that I told you about him yesterday.* Such use of a "resumptive pronoun" may not be a marker of some dialect, but it is common nonstandard English.
10. *I haven't got any.* Fine in all dialects of English.
11. *We've some money for you.* British.
12. *I asked him if he could come out and play.* Probably fine in all dialects of English.
13. *I asked him could he come out and play:* Black English indirect question formation.
14. *I know where he:* ungrammatical in all dialects of English.
15. *It is a lot of love in that house.* Black English *it* for standard English existential *there*.

Exercise 6. Projects will vary greatly.
Exercise 7: Responses will very greatly.

Exercise 8: Senses of the term "grammar":

1. You shouldn't use contractions in a formal paper: PRESCRIPTIVE; GLOBAL. The form of the rule gives it away: it's advice about how to use the language, so it's prescriptive. Contractions are basically phonological, so it's a "global" rule.
2. English has irregular past tenses: DESCRIPTIVE; NARROW.
3. *Chopped down* is a phrase but *down the* isn't: DESCRIPTIVE; NARROW.
4. Subject-verb agreement: DESCRIPTIVE; NARROW.
5. Words beginning with the "ng" sound are impossible in English: DESCRIPTIVE; GLOBAL (since phonological).
6. *Less* is used with mass nouns, *fewer* with count nouns: DESCRIPTIVE; NARROW.
7. No gender agreement in English adjectives: DESCRIPTIVE; NARROW.
8. Adjectives precede nouns: DESCRIPTIVE; NARROW.
9. Prohibition against *ain't:* PRESCRIPTIVE; presumably GLOBAL since the prohibition applies to a single word. That is, it's a vocabulary fact. But arguably NARROW since *ain't* is a common way in non-standard dialects of English to make a sentence negative; in some of these dialects, *ain't* supplants auxiliary verbs *be, have,* and *do: She ain't here* (be), *She ain't never seen you before* (have), *She ain't leave yet* (do).
10. *Bull, ram,* etc. contain "[+masculine]" meaning feature: DESCRIPTIVE; GLOBAL.
11. Verb agreement with nearest subject: To the extent that this is a matter of prescriptive concern, this is a PRESCRIPTIVE rule; NARROW.

Exercise 9:

Some paraphrases, for *Mary bought a blue dress for Susie,* not exhausting the set:

1. Mary bought a dress that was blue for Susie.
2. Mary bought a dress which was blue for Susie.
3. Mary bought Susie a blue dress.
4. Mary bought Susie a dress that was blue.
5. Mary bought Susie a dress which was blue.
6. A blue dress was bought by Mary for Susie.
7. A blue dress was bought Susie by Mary.
8. A dress that was blue was bought by Mary for Susie.
9. Mary bought a dress for Susie. The dress was blue.
10. Mary bought Susie a dress. The dress was blue.
11. Mary bought Susie a dress. It was blue.
12. For Susie, Mary bought a blue dress.
13. For Susie, Mary bought a dress that was blue.
14. Blue was the color of a dress that Mary bought for Susie.
15. Blue was the color of a dress that Mary bought Susie.
16. Mary bought something for Susie, a blue dress.
17. Mary bought something that was blue for Susie, a dress.

Excluded from the paraphrase set are forms like these:

≠ 18. What Mary bought for Susie was a blue dress.
≠ 19. It was a blue dress that Mary bought for Susie.
≠ 20. The dress that Mary bought for Susie was blue.
≠ 21. The one who bought a blue dress for Susie was Mary

These are excluded because they entail uniqueness while the original sentence (*Mary bought a blue dress for Susie*) doesn't. Examples (18) and (19) each entail that Mary bought just one thing for Susie (in the current universe of discourse), and (20 and 21) each entail that Mary bought just one dress for Susie.

Chapter Two. The Structure of English Sound.

Exercise 1:

1. (e) Silent letter, but still one that "does some work," of course, since it signals the pronunciation of the preceding vowel letter.

2. (a) The letter 'n' has two pronunciations, [n] and "ng" (i.e., [ŋ]).

3. (b) Different spellings represent the same sound.

4. (a) A given letter ('c') has two pronunciations.

5. (a) The spelling 'th' has a "voiced" pronunciation in *this* and a voiceless pronunciation in *think*. Note that the use of two successive letters to represent one sound is a second way that 'th' deviates from the phonetic ideal.

Exercise 2:

1. 4 [tæks]   2. 4 [mɪst]   3. 4 [šʌvz]   4. 3 [sin]
5. 5 [fɪlɪp]   6. 4 [mʌðr̩]   7. 3 [θɔt]   8. 4 [batl̩]

Exercise 3:

1. voiced.   2. voiceless.   3. voiced.   4. voiceless.   5. voiced.   6. voiced.
7. voiceless.   8. voiced.   9. voiced.

Exercise 4:

oceans, lucky, through (threw), television, seeps, chat, bathes, machines, looked, often, math, nippy, bud (Bud), bingo.

Exercise 5: [z], [ŋ], [t], [z], [č], [ɟ], [k], [θ], [š], [ə],[s], [i], [i], [z].

Exercise 6: [its], [no], [ni], [mæst], [bɛt], [lɪk], [lʊk], [šuz], [kat], [pʌtəd], [opənd], [wæks], [simz], [rabd], [soŋz] or [saŋz], [rið], [kɔt] or [kat], [hɛlpt], [irz], [fæsənd], [ošənz], [əknaləj] or [æknaləj].

Exercise 7: [ɟoyfəl], [mayn], [klawn], [ay], [ənɔyz], [ərawnd], [lɔndri] or [landri], [məlayn], [ɪči], [byuti], [grawnd], [dray], [steyd].

4

Exercise 8:

A.   words, shuttle, cotton, comfort, worthy, sitting (sittin').

B.   [mɾθfl̩] or [mɾθfəl or [mɾθfʊl]], [hɾd], [hart], bɾdənz] or [bɾdn̩z],
       [sæʔn̩], [mɛtl̩].

Exercise 9:

Bill, the native English speaker, will have a harder time learning about Japanese vowel length than
Akeo, the native Japanese speaker, will have learning about English vowel length. The reason is
that Bill will have to learn to hear and recognize long vowels as contrasted with short ones, a
distinction that is below his level of conscious awareness, since in English the short-long
distinction is automatic rather than psychologically salient. Akeo, on the other hand, has it easy; he
can merely put aside and ignore the Japanese vowel length distinction in the process of learning
English, since that distinction has no psychological relevance for English. Moreover, Akeo may
accurately hear English vowels that are phonetically long or short and may reproduce their length
accurately, since he is accustomed to the difference.

Exercise 10:

	bean	badge	writes	con	prime	pond	post
Underlying:	/biːn/	/bæːʝ/	/rayːts/	/kaːn/	/prayːm/	/paːnd/	/poːst/
Phonetic:	[bĩːn]	[bæːʝ]	[rayts]	[kʰãːn]	[pʰrãyːm]	[pʰãːnd]	[pʰost]

Exercise 11:

A.   It appears on the basis of this data that [ɫ] occurs word finally, while [l] occurs word-
       initially.

B.   It appears on the basis of this data that [ɫ] occurs word finally or before central or back
       vowels, while [l] occurs elsewhere, i.e., before front vowels.

Exercise 12:

1.   [s] and [š] are allophones of one phoneme in Korean, because they are phonetically
       similar and in complementary distribution: [š] occurs only before [i], while [s] always
       occurs elsewhere.

Exercise 13:

1.   /o/ becomes [ɔ] before a nasal.
2.   A consonant becomes nasalized after a nasal.
3.   A voiced stop becomes a fricative between vowels.
4.   An alveolar stop becomes bilabial before a bilabial sound.
5.   /r/ deletes word finally or before a consonant.

Exercise 14:

1. $V \rightarrow [\text{-voice}] \; / \; \underset{[\text{-voice}]}{C} \; \underline{\quad} \; \underset{[\text{-voice}]}{C}$

2. $[\text{+nasal}] \rightarrow [\text{+syllabic}] \; / \; \#\underline{\quad}[\text{+stop}]$

3. $/l/ \rightarrow 0 \; / \; \underset{\underline{\quad}C}{\#}$

4. $\underset{[\text{+voice}]}{C} \rightarrow 0 \; / \; \underset{[\text{+voice}]}{C} \; \underline{\quad} \; \#$

Exercise 15:

A.

1. Where is my brown alligator wallet?   or   Where is my brown alligator wallet?

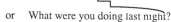

2. What were you doing last night?   or   What were you doing last night?

3. He may be small, but he is fast.

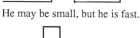

4. I'll show him a thing or two.

B.   At the end.

Additional Exercise:

1. [d] and [ð] are allophones of one phoneme in complementary distribution: [ð] always occurs between vowels, whereas [d] always occurs elsewhere.

2. [b] and [β] are allophones of one phoneme in complementary distribution: [β] always occurs between vowels, whereas [b] always occurs elsewhere.

3. [ɣ] and [g] are allophones of one phoneme in complementary distribution: [ɣ] always occurs between vowels, whereas [g] always occurs elsewhere.

4. Voiced stops become fricatives between vowels: $\begin{bmatrix} \text{+voice} \\ \text{+stop} \end{bmatrix} \rightarrow [\text{+fric}] \; / \; V\underline{\quad}V$

Chapter Three. The Structure of English Words

Exercise 1:   grand - mother, play - ful - ly, desk - s, Oklahoma,
                     algebra - ic, act - iv -ity, always, un - happi - ly

Exercise 2:

A.   nitajua, tumejua.

B.   Morphemes: [baš] 'head'; [lar] 'plural'; [da] 'in (the)'; [kuš] 'bird';
                         [dost] 'friend'; [yaš] 'age'; [kol] 'arm'; [pul] 'stamp'

         'friend': [dost]
         'in the arm': [kolda]
         'in the stamp': [pulda]
         'arms': [kollar]

Exercise 3:

1.   All lexical, because they have meanings easily expressible as definitions or by pointing out examples of what they refer to, and because they don't express meanings that are common or obligatory.

2.   Lexical, because its meaning is easily expressible in a dictionary definition and it doesn't express a common or obligatory meaning.

3.   Grammatical, since it is common and obligatory (all sentences require tense).

4.   Grammatical, since its meaning is not easily defiinable and it expresses a relation in a sentence: all these -ing words are gerunds (which makes them nouns) which interact grammatically with other expressions: -'s, poetry, the.

5.   Probably best called grammatical, although it is not common or obligatory, because its "meaning" is not easily expressible in a dictionary definition; rather, it functions to make words verbs, a 'grammatical' function.

6.   Arguably lexical, since its meaning is easily definable in dictionary terms ('in such-and-such manner') and is not particularly commonly expressed (as compared with, say, tense; but note that it is common, nearly ubiquitous, among adverbs); BUT arguably grammatical since it functions to make words adverbs, a 'grammatical' function.

7.   Lexical, since its meaning is easily defined in dictionary terms--"possession"--and is not particularly commonly expressed.

8.   Grammatical: although it is not particularly commonly expressed, it carries a meaning which is not easily defined in dictionary terms or ostensively, and the meaning has to do with intra-sentential relations rather than denoting objects, events, properties, etc., in the world.

Exercise 4:

Inflectional morphemes in English occur at the right-most periphery of words, outside any derivational morphemes.

Singlehandedly, drunkenness, and *excitedly* appear to be counterexamples, since the inflectional morphemes *-ed* and *-en* occur to the left of the derivational morphemes *-ly* and *-ness.* The generalization about order of inflectional and derivational morphemes threfore needs an amendment. while generally correct, it is subject to the countervailing influence of rules of word-building that have to do with particular morphemes. The adverb-forming suffix *-ly* and the noun-forming suffix *-ness* attach to adjectives; some adjectives are formed by attaching *-ed* (or *-en: drunkenly*) to a verb root.

Exercise 5:

The adjective-forming suffix *-able* goes only with transitive verbs, i.e., those which take direct objects (roughly definable as noun phrases following them, but see Chapter 7):

1. He washed the clothes   The clothes are washable
    They painted the walls   The walls are paintable
    She sliced the bagels   The bagels are sliceable
    The team won the game   The game is winnable

Intransitive verbs--those which do not permit a following noun phrase--do not tolerate *-able:*

2. He slept   *He slept the baby   *He is sleepable
                                                    *The baby is sleepable

    She smiled   *She smiled the porter   *She is smileable
                                                          *The porter is smileable

    My car goes   *My car goes town   *The car is goable
                                                      *Town is goable

The examples above reveal why: adjectives with *-able* make predications about (say something about) the direct object noun phrases (e.g., *the clothes*). Sentences whose main verb doesn't allow a direct object noun phrase contain no word the *-able* adjective could make a predication about.

Within the subclass of transitive verbs, *-able* seems productive.

Exercise 6:

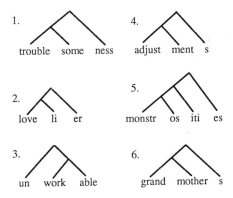

1.
trouble some ness

4.
adjust ment s

2.
love li er

5.
monstr os iti es

3.
un work able

6.
grand mother s

Exercise 7:

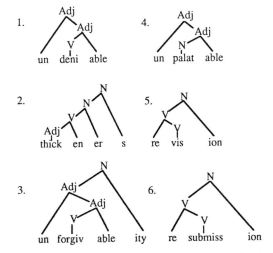

1.
Adj
  Adj
  V
un deni able

4.
Adj
  Adj
  N
un palat able

2.
N
N
V
Adj
thick en er s

5.
N
V
V
re vis ion

3.
N
Adj
  Adj
  V
un forgiv able ity

6.
N
V
V
re submiss ion

In tree 1, *deni* is the verb *deny,* in tree 3, *forgiv* is the verb *forgive,* in tree 4, *palat* is the noun *palate,* in tree 5, *vis* is the bound verb root meaning 'see,' and in tree 6 *submiss* is the verb *submit.*

9

Exercise 8:

N [N base | N ball]

N [N' [N basket | N ball] | s]

V [V [N' [N wall | N paper]] | ed]

Exercise 9:

N V+ -er = 'that which Vs by means of N': 1. vacuum cleaner; 4, pressure cooker.
N V+ -er = 'that which Vs powered by N': 7, gas mower; 8, windsurfer
V+ -ing N = 'N which/who Vs': 2, polarizing filter; 5, cleaning woman; 9, cleaning solution; 11, magnifying glass.
V N = 'that which/the one who Vs N': 3, breakwater; 6, killjoy; 10, pickpocket; 12, know-it-all.

Exercise 10:

yuppie: acronym (from **y**oung **u**rban **p**rofessional).
workaholic: reanalyzing morpheme boundaries: *alcoholic* reinterpreted as *alc - oholic.*
sellathon: reanalyzing morpheme boundaries: *marathon* reinterpreted as *mar - athon.*
walkman: compounding; also a brand name turned into a common noun.
modem: blending of **mod**ulate + **dem**odulate.
a steal: functional shift (zero-derivation).
to badmouth: compounding.

Exercise 11:

From the list given in (29), presumably the following idioms are metaphoric in origin, all involving generalizations from some particular instance:

To throw in the towel (from the traditional signal of capitulation in a boxing match).
Hold your horses (the idiom meaning 'wait' generalizes from a particular instance of waiting).
To put one's best foot forward(unclear in origin, but it may be that this idiom, meaning 'present one's best feature(s),' is also a generalization from a particular instance of doing that).
To sell down the river (from a much-feared betrayal of trust during the slavery era).
To eat one's hat (another generalization from a particular. *Eat one's hat* is a member of the same family of idiomatic expressions as *monkey's uncle* and *when hell freezes over:* expressions used to imply that some proposition is extremely unlikely to be true. Given a proposition P that a speaker believes is ridiculous or highly improbable, the speaker can say *If P, I will eat my hat/I'm a monkey's uncle* or *P will eventuate when hell freezes over* to imply that P is highly improbable. The inference that P is unlikely arises from the meaning of *if..(then)* and the unlikeliness of eating one's hat, being a monkey's uncle, or hell freezing over.).
To put one's foot in one's mouth (another generalization from a particular, one way of being egregiously awkward so as to offend).
To throw one's weight around (a physical manifestation of inappropriate aggressiveness).

Exercise 12:

The pronunciations of past tense -ed are [t], [d], and [əd] (or [ɪd]).

Exercise 13:

[t] occurs after voiceless sounds except [t]; [d] occurs after voiced sounds except [d]; and [əd] occurs after alveolar stops ([t] and [d]).

Exercise 14:

1. [m] and [mw].
2. [mw] occurs before vowels; [m] occurs before consonants.
3. Yes, it is complementary.
4. [ninamfundisha].
5. [ninamweleza].

Exercise 15:

A. *washed:*

    Underlying form: /wašd/
                        ⇓   Devoicing rule, i.e., /d/ -> [-voice] / [-voice]__#
    Phonetic form: [wašt]

    dried:

    Underlying form: /drayd/
                        ⇓   (No rule applies)
    Phonetic form: [drayd]

    admitted:

    Underlying form: /ədmɪtd/
                        ⇓   [ə]-insertion rule, i.e., 0 -> [ə] / $\begin{bmatrix} \text{+alveolar} \\ \text{+stop} \end{bmatrix}$ __d
                      [ədmɪtəd]

    designed:

    Underlying form: /dizaynd/
                        ⇓   (No rule applies)
    Phonetic form: [dizaynd]

11

decided:

Underlying form: /disaydd/

Phonetic form: [disaydəd]

$$\text{[ə]-insertion rule, i.e., } 0 \to \text{[ə]} \Bigg/ \begin{bmatrix} +\text{alveolar} \\ +\text{stop} \end{bmatrix} \_\_\text{d}$$

B.   With basic allomorph [-əd]:

Underlying forms: /wašəd/, /drayəd/, /ədmɪtəd/, /dizaynəd/, /disaydəd/

Rules: Two are needed, one to delete the [ə] in /wašəd/, /drayəd/, and /dizaynəd/, and one to devoice the final [d] in words like *washed,* whose roots end with a voiceless sound other than [t]. The [ə]-deletion rule will delete any [ə] that is between a pair of sounds at the end of a word EXCEPT a pair of alveolar stops.

/wašəd/
  ↓   [ə]-deletion rule
wašd
  ↓   final [-d] devoicing rule
[wašt]

/drayəd/
  ↓   [ə]-deletion rule
[drayd]

/ədmɪtəd/
    (No rules apply)
[ədmɪtəd]

/dizaynəd/
  ↓   [ə]-deletion rule
[dizaynd]

/disaydəd/
    (No rules apply)
[disaydəd]

C.   a.   With basic allomorph [-t]:

Underlying forms: /wašt/, /drayt/, /ədmɪtt/, /dizaynt/, /disaydt/

Rules: [ə]-insertion, just as in A above except that the environment will be "between an alveolar stop and a [t]," and a rule to voice the word-final [t] after voiced sounds.

$$\text{[ə]-insertion: } 0 \to \text{[ə]} \Bigg/ \begin{bmatrix} +\text{alveolar} \\ +\text{stop} \end{bmatrix} \_\_\text{t}$$

Voicing rule: t -> [+voice] / [+voice]__#

/wašt/ -> [wašt] (No rule applies)

/drayt/ -> (Voicing rule) [drayd]

/ədmɪtt/ -> ([ə]-insertion) [ədmɪtət] -> (Voicing rule) [ədmɪləd]

/dizaynt/ -> (Voicing rule) [dizaynd]

/disaydt/ -> ([ə]-insertion) [disaydət] -> (Voicing rule) [disaydəd]

NOTE: In *admitted* and *decided*, the voicing rule voices the final [t] because it follows a voiced sound, the vowel [ə]. This seems to explain why the allomorph of the past tense morpheme ends in [d] rather than [t] when it follows a vowel; the other descriptions, with [-d] and [-əd] as basic allomorphs, merely assume the voiced [d] underlyingly. HOWEVER--

b.   *Carrot* and *target* show that the /t/-based analysis is wrong, because, like many words, they end with a [t] after a voiced sound, e.g, a vowel. So the description above cannot be maintained, since [t]s don't generally get voiced after vowels word-finally.

Exercise 16:

A.   [s], [z], and [əz].

B.   [əz] occurs after the sibilants ; [s]occurs after voiceless non-sibilant sounds; and[z] occurs after voiced non-sibilants.

C.   With [z] as the basic allomorph:

Underlying forms of typical plural nouns:

sizes: /sayzz/   *cups:* /kʌpz/   *rugs:* /rʌgz/

Phonological rules:

A [ə]-insertion rule very like the one used in the analysis of the past tense, and a devoicing rule likewise similar to the devoicing rule of the past tense.

[ə]-insertion rule: 0 -> [ə] / [+sibilant]__[z]#

Devoicing rule: /z/ -> [-voice] / [-voice]__#

Derivations:

/sayzz/ -> [sayzəz]   (via the [ə]-insertion rule)

/kʌpz/-> [kʌps]   (via the devoicing rule)

/rʌgz/ -> [rʌgz]   (No rule applies.)

D.   With [əz] as the basic allomorph:

Underlying forms of typical plural nouns:

sizes: /sayzəz/   *cups:* /kʌpəz/   *rugs:* /rʌgəz/

Phonological rules:

A [ə]-deletion rule, and the same devoicing rule posited above.

[ə]-deletion rule: Delete a [ə] between a pair of sounds at the end of a word unless it is between a pair of sibilants.

Devoicing rule: /z/ -> [-voice] / [-voice]__#

Derivations:

/sayzəz/ -> [sayzəz] (No change)

/kʌpəz/-> kʌpz (via the [ə]-deletion rule) -> [kʌps] (via the devoicing rule)

/rʌgəz/ -> [rʌgz] (via the [ə]-deletion rule)

With [-s] as the basic allomorph:

Underlying forms of typical plural nouns:

sizes: /sayzs/   *cups:* /kʌps/   *rugs:* /rʌgs/

Phonological rules:

A [ə]-insertion rule and a voicing rule.

[ə]-insertion rule: 0 -> [ə] / [+sibilant]__[s]#

Voicing rule: /s/ -> [+voice] / [+voice]__#

Derivations:

/sayzs/ -> ([ə]-insertion rule) sayzəs -> (Voicing rule) [sayzəz]

/kʌps/-> [kʌps] (No change)

/rʌgs/ -> [rʌgz] (Voicing rule)

NOTE: This last description suffers from the same failing as the analogous description for the past tense morpheme: the voicing rule incorrectly predicts that words like *boss* and *miss* would be impossible, since they have a voiceless [s] after a voiced sound (a vowel).

14

Exercise 17:

Underlying forms for the morphemically simple words:

/məlɪgn/, /sɪgn/, /rizɪgn/

(using "ɪ", and not worrying about the [ay] / [ɪ] alternation)

Underlying forms for the morphemically complex words:

/məlɪgnənt/, /sɪgnəl/, /rizɪgneyšən/

Phonological rule: /g/ → Ø / [n]___#

Exercise 18:

A.   Underlying forms for the morphemically simple words:

/ayæmb/, /bamb/, /krʌmb/

Underlying forms for the morphemically complex words:

/ayæmbɪk/, /bambard/, /krʌmbḷ/

Phonological rule: /b/ → Ø /[m]___#

B.   The underlying forms for *thumb* and *tomb* are different from those for *iamb* and *bomb*, because there is no evidence from related words (e.g., *thumbnail, tombstone*) that *thumb* and *tomb* underlyingly contain a final /b/. (The phonetic forms for these words ([θʌmneyl], [tʰumston]) lack phonetic [b]s.)

Exercise 19:

By verb agreement, as in *Fish are tasty* as opposed to *Fish is tasty;* by the form of "demonstrative determiners" (*these, those* vs. *this, that*); or by the presence of a plural-denoting "quantifier" (*all, lots, many,* etc.), as in *I can see many of the fish.*

Exercise 20:

dive:	in the [ay] → [o] class, like *ride*
shed:	in the [0] class, like *cut*
sweep:	in the [i] → [ɛ] + suffixed [−t] class, like *sleep*
rend:	in the [d] → [t] class, like *bend*
weave:	in the [i] → [o] class, like *steal*
throw:	in the [o] → [u] class, like *blow*
know:	in the [o] → [u] class, like *blow*

15

Exercise 21:

[æ] → [ɛ], as in *man -> men*
[ʊ] → [ɪ], as in *woman -> women*
[ən], as in *children , oxen* (taking the form [čɪldr-] as an allomorph of the root)
[∅], as in *sheep, fish, deer, trout*
[ə], as in *data, criteria*
[ay], as in *alumni*
[aw] → [ay], as in *mice*
[ɪs] → [iz], as in *analyses, hypotheses*
[ʊ] → [i], as in *foot -> feet*
[u] → [i], as in *tooth -> teeth*
[ə] → [i] (or [ay]), as in *larva -> larvae , alumna -> alumnae*
[əs] → [i], as in *stimulus -> stimuli*

Additional Exercises:

1. *Un-* is less restricted, attaching to both native Anglo-Saxon English words (*unbreakable*) and to many Latin or Romance borrowings (*undecipherable , unimaginable*), whereas *in-* is largely restricted to words of clear Latin or Romance origin (*inconceivable, indecisive, inarticulate*); forms like **inbreakable* and **inhealthy* are not possible. In addition, many words with *in-* are marginally acceptable with *un-* substituted. To many speakers, *unconceivable* doesn't seem to be a totally impossible formation. However, *un-* words are impossible with *in-* (**inbreakable, *inimaginable*).

    However, the test for productivity is freedom of combination to make new words, not the size of the domain in which the morpheme in question occurs. Testing Latin or Romance stems with *un-* and *in-* attached to form new words suggests that *un-* is more productive, as well as less restricted. *Untelevised* (e.g., *the untelevised tapes*), *untelephoned, uncaloric, uncarcinogenic, undemonic* all seem better than the corresponding forms with *in-* (**intelevised,* etc.).

2. Exercise 2 will have a wide range of answers.

3. Compounds, because of their stress pattern:

    stock market, stock market analyst, cheesecake, convenience store, wood shop, paper route, paper route collection book, mud pie

4. 1. "Undersegmentation": the child, hearing utterances like "I'm going to change you", hypothesizes a single morpheme *changeyou.*

    2. "Mis-segmentation": the child, hearing "an apple," mis-locates the morpheme boundary.

    3. Undersegmentation.

    4. "Oversegmentation": the child interprets the word-final [z] as the plural.

5. Overextending the range of a morpheme which occurs only in a limited environment.

6. All cases of overgeneralization of regular past and plural allomorphs to irregular verbs and nouns.

5. Allomorphs, with meanings:

> 'finger': [onit], [onid]
> 'chair': [rek]
> 'road': [stel]
> 'button': [tap], [tab]
> 'mountain': [fliz]
> 'chain': [elup]
> 'sky': [surk], [surg]

Underlying forms: /onid/, /tab/, /surg/.

Phonological rule: [+stop] -> [-voice]/__#

17

Chapter Four. "Parts of Speech"

Exercise 1:

1. *table:* N (takes plural, possessive; occurs after articles); also V (takes tense--*they tabled the motion*).
2. *create:* V (takes tense). Not N (can't take plural, possessive; can't occur with articles).
3. *concise:* Not N (can't take plural or possessive--*concises, concise's* ; can't occur after articles at sentence-end (*I bought a concise.*). Not V (can't take tense--*concised*).
4. *enslave:* V (takes tense). Not N (can't occur with plural or possessive; can't occur with articles.).
5. *attack:* Both N (takes plural, article, possessive) and V (takes tense).
6. *visualize:* V (takes tense). Not N.
7. *skin:* Both N (takes plural, possessive; occurs with article) and V (takes tense).
8. *partition:* Both N (takes plural, article, possessive) and V (as V: *They partitioned the room into little cubicles*)
9. *destroy:* V only (takes tense); not N (fails plural, article, possessive tests).
10. *person:* N only.
11. *appear:* V only.
12. *visualization:* N only.

Exercise 2:

blind: A set-denoter (like *red*) because we can conceive of a set of blind people or animals.

short: Relative to noun (like *large* (a short walk is shorter than a short drive). Not relative to the user (the *good* type), because shortness is not a particularly subjective judgment.

expensive: Relative to noun (expensive milkshakes are less costly than expensive cars), but not relative to user, because people agree, by and large, about what is expensive (even those who can afford a Rolls Royce agree it is an expensive car).

married: Set-denoting.

transparent: Set-denoting.

round: Set-denoting.

interesting: Relative both to the modified noun and to the user (though there may be argument about whether it is relative to the modifed noun);

famous: Set-denoting (people agree, by and large, about who or what is famous).

Exercise 3:

beautiful: Adj. Positive attributes: occurs between Article and Noun (*the beautiful sunset*); occurs in slot (Art) N is ___ (*The sunset is beautiful*). Negative attributes: cannot occur with plural (*beautifuls*); cannot occur with possessive (*beautiful's*).

handsome: Adj. Fits all positive and negative attributes.

stinky: Adj. Fits all positive and negative attributes.

house: Not an adjective: Although it fits the first positive attribute for adjectives (*the house painter, the house wall*), it fails the negative attributes (it can occur with a plural--*houses* --and with a possessive--*house's*).

tree:	Not an adjective, just like the previous case.
behind:	Not an adjective. Fits neither of the positive attributes.
disk:	Not an adjective, by the negative attributes (*disks, disk's*).
circular:	Adjective, fitting both the positive attributes and the negative attributes. (Assume that the noun *circular* ('leaflet') is a homonym.)
world:	Not an adjective. Fits the first positive attribute (*the world congress*), but fails the negative attributes (*worlds, world's*).
legal:	Adj. Fits the positive attributes (*a legal analysis; your problem is legal, not ethical*), and both the negative attributes (**legals, *legal's*).
criminal:	Somewhat problematical. Seems adjectival, because it fits both the positive attributes. But it fails the negative attributes, since it can take plurals and possessives. This may be due to cross-classification; that is, there may be two homonyms with the form *criminal,* one an adjective, one a noun.
constitutional:	Adj, under both the positive attributes and the negative attributes.
up:	By our criteria, *up* is an adjective. It possesses the first positive attribute if you accept expressions like *an up person;* and expressions like *the kite is up* and *the notice is up* are unquestionably OK. Since *up* can't take a plural or possessive, it possesses both the positive and the negative attributes.
	Up is, of course, cross-classified as a preposition (*up the stairs, up the tree*). (It is also cross-classified as a particle; see p. 158-159.)
quickly:	Not an adjective. Possesses neither positive attribute (**the quickly man, the man is quickly*), and does not take plural or possessive suffix (**quicklys, quickly's*).
very:	While *very* appears to possess the first positive attribute, as in *the very book* , this use is probaby a homonym of the intensifier *very,* and *very* possesses neither of the negative attributes (**verys, *very's*).
sleeping:	By criteria (9) and (10), *sleeping* is an adjective: *the sleeping cat, the cat is sleeping; *sleepings, *sleeping's* (although it should be noted that some speakers may find use with a possessive OK: *Sleeping's benefit is good health*). But see the discussion later in the chapter (p. 137-139), where it is suggested that *sleeping* is not an adjective, but a verb.
exciting:	Adjective: *the exciting film, the film is exciting; *excitings, *exciting's.*
Exercise 4:	Discussed in the text.

Exercise 5:

1.   Denominal: No manner adverb paraphrase (**That operation is unnecessary in a medical manner*), but has the proper denominal kind of paraphrase: *That operation is unnecessary from the perspective of medicine.*

2. Denominal: *Sen. Blowhard's amendment is unsound from the perspective of the Constitution.*

3. Probably best labeled an intensifier, since it is clearly not denominal (**We had a time last night that was awesome from the perspective of totality*) and the manner adverb version is at least questionable and perhaps not a paraphrase of the original sentence (*?We had a time last night that was awesome in a total manner*).

4. Denominal: *Eskimo verbs are complex from the perspective of morphology.*

5. Manner: *President Nixon may have been dishonest in a criminal manner.* Not denominal, because the meaning isn't that Pres. Nixon may have been dishonest from the perspective of crime.

6. Intensifier: Clearly not denominal (**...difficult from the perspective of impossibility*). Not manner either, since the meaning isn't that they were difficult in an impossible manner. By elimination of the alternatives, *impossibly* must be an intensifier here.

7. Manner: *Sheila grabbed Joan's cards is a playful manner.*

8. Denominal: *Claiming a tax deduction without a receipt is questionable from the perspective of law.*

9. Manner: *The judge peered down at the witness in a skeptical manner.*

10. Intensifier: Not denominal (**...cool from the perspective of ??*); not manner, since an attempt at a paraphrase like *cool in an extreme manner* really isn't a paraphrase (note that the expression *for me* can't go with the "paraphrase").

Exercise 6:

1. *strangely:* Manner (*Max smiled strangely = Max smiled in a strange manner*); also sentence adverb (*Strangely, Max arrived late = That Max arrived late is strange*).

2. *politically:* Denominal (*The attache's idea was politically unsound = ...unsound from the perspective of politics*); manner also (*He is behaving very politically = He is behaving in a very political manner*).

3. *beautifully:* Manner (*She sang beautifully = she sang in a beautiful manner*).

4. *possessively:* Manner (*She held his arm possessively = ...in a possessive manner*).

5. *literally:* Both a sentence adverb (*I was literally sweating through my shirt = That I was sweating through my shirt is literal* --that is, '...is literally true') and a manner adverb (*She took what they said literally = She took what they said in a literal manner*).

6. *undoubtedly:* Sentence adverb (*You will undoubtedly arrive late = that you will arrive late is undoubted*).

7. *today:* Sentence adverb (*They are leaving today = Their leaving is today*).

8. *statistically:* Denominal (*These figures are statistically insignificant = These figures are insignificant from the perspective of statistics*).

20

9. *demographically:* Denominal (*Demographically, our new advertising campaign makes a lot of sense = From the perspective of demographics, ...*)

10. *quite:* Intensifier. Has none of the paraphrases which can identify it as any of the other types.

Exercise 7:

1. *heartily:* manner adverb; *government:* noun; *rapidly:* manner adverb; *systematically:* manner adverb; *usually:* sentence adverb; *sometimes:* sentence adverb; *inexpedient:* adjective.

2. *has:* verb; *orderly:* adjective; *football:* noun; *stay:* verb; *disorderly:* adjective; *prose:* noun.

3. *are:* verb; *technologically:* denominal adverb; *advance:* noun; *razor:* noun; *blade:* noun; *stainless:* adjective; *steel:* noun.

Exercise 8:

Fourscore and seven (Q) years ago, our forefathers brought forth on *this* (Dem) continent *a* (Art) new nation, conceived in liberty and dedicated to *the* (Art) proposition that *all* (Q) men are created equal. Now we are engaged in *a* (Art) great civil war, testing whether *that* (Dem) nation, or *any* (Q) nation so conceived and so dedicated, can long endure. We are met on *a* (Art) great battlefield of *that* (Dem) war. We have come to dedicate *a* (Art) portion of *that* (Dem) field, as *a* (Art) final resting place for *those* (Dem; here used as a pronoun) who here gave their lives that *that* (Dem) nation might live. It is altogether fitting and proper that we should do *this* (Dem; here used as a pronoun).

Exercise 9:

A. 1. "past" participle (verbal)
    2. gerund
    3. "past" participle (verbal)
    4. present participle (verbal; it's a complement construction)
    5. present participle (adjectival)
    6. gerund (note *washing machine* is a noun compound, meaning 'machine for washing')
    7. present participle (verbal; note the paraphrase *As I was leaving town,...*)
    8. gerund
    9. present participle (verbal)
    10. Both words are adjectival past participles.

B. In one reading (meaning), it means that Joe was in the process of entertaining. This is a verbal use. In the other reading, it means that Joe had the characteristic of being entertaining, an adjectival use.

21

Exercise 10:

A.   1. exclusive.   2. inclusive.   3. inclusive.   4. exclusive.   5. exclusive, on the assumption that a tomato cannot be red and yellow at the same time.   6. exclusive.   7. inclusive.

B.   1.   The second clause is not contrary to a built-up "discourse model" in which football running backs must be big or fast, preferably both.

2.   Clause order clashes with normal event order.

3.   There is only one difference between the clauses; *but* requires two.

4.   There is no mutual relevance between the clauses connected by *and.*

Exercise 11:

1.   The antecedent is *several of the fans,* not just *the fans,* because the meaning of *they* is 'several of the fans,' not '(all) the fans.'

2.   The antecedent is *the reporters covering the story.*

3.   The antecedent is *the possibility that snow might slow down our trip.*

4.   The antecedent is *anyone.* An example interesting from the perspective of sexism in the language. The prescriptively correct pronoun is the masculine *he,* agreeing with the singular *anyone,* but many speakers use the gender-neutral *they* to agree with the gender-neutral *anyone,* in order to avoid the inherent masculine gender of *he.* This issue is touched on again in Chapter Five.

5.   The antecedent is *English.* An interesting feature of this example is that the antecedent follows, rather than precedes, the pronoun that refers to it. This is less common than the order ANTECEDENT...PRONOUN, but is by no means rare.

6.   The antecedent is *swing the chain into the chest of his pursuer,* which isn't present--in exactly that form--in the example sentence. The verb *swung,* of course is "really" *swing + PAST,* and the actual pronoun is not *doing so,* but *do so,* with *-ing* being a piece of verbal morphology attached to this "pro-verb phrase."

Exercise 12:

he (ant: *Max*); he (ant: *he*); his (ant: *he*); their (ant: *his evening refreshments*); his (ant: *he*); thus (ant: *in the distant left-field stands, alone, with an empty seat to either side*); its (ant: *a voice*); this (ant: *shout "we want Sims"*); him (ant: *Max*); they (ant: *the home team*); it (ant: *the game*); he (ant: *Max*); himself (ant: *he*); his (ant: *he*).

Exercise 13:

Both sentences contain a verb + particle sequence. But only the first contains a movable particle (as can be seen from the position of *on*). Semantically, the verb + particle sequence in (a) is paraphrasable as "excite" or "intoxicate", with *turn* having no relation to the meaning of the ordinary verb turn (except through a metaphoric extension); the verb + particle sequence in (b) has a meaning much closer to that of the ordinary verb *turn*, though distinct from it. The particle in (b) is not movable rightward (≠*I turned him on*), but, more importantly, it is not movable leftward along with the following noun expression (pronoun, here: ≠*On him, I turned*). This makes it a particle, not a preposition. The difference in interpretation between these two verb + particle expressions, with the same verb and particle, underscores the idiomatic nature of verb + particle constructions.

Additional Exercise:

When [subordinate conjunction] in [prep] the [art] course [noun] of [prep] human [adj] events [noun], *it* [extraposition marker; see Chapter Eight] becomes [verb] necessary [adj] for [prep*] one [quantifier] people [noun] to [infinitive marker] dissolve [verb] the [art] political [adj] bands [noun] which [relative pronoun] have [aux; verb] connected [verb; past participle] them [pronoun] with [prep] another [quantifier], and [coordinate conjunction] to [inf. marker] assume [verb] among [prep] the [art] powers [noun] of [prep] the [art] earth [noun] the [art] separate [adj] and [coord. conj.] equal [adj] station [noun] to [prep] which [relative pro] the [art] laws [noun] of [prep] nature [noun] and [coord. conj.] of [prep] nature's [noun] God [noun] entitle [verb] them [pro], a [art] decent [adj] respect [noun] to [prep] the [art] opinions [noun] of [prep] mankind [noun] requires [verb] that [complementizer; subordinate conjunction] they [pro] should [aux; modal] declare [verb] the [art] causes [noun] which [rel. pro] impel [verb] them [pro] to [prep] the [art] separation [noun].

We [pro] hold [verb] these [determiner; demonstrative] truths [noun] to [inf. marker] be [verb] self-evident [adj], that [comp] all [quant] men [noun] are [verb; aux] created [verb; past participle] equal [adj], that [comp] they [pro] are [verb; aux] endowed [verb; past participle] by [prep] their [possessive determiner] creator [noun] with [prep] certain [adj] inalienable [adj] rights [noun], that [comp] among [prep] these [demonstrative] are [verb] life [noun], liberty [noun], and [coord. conj.] the [art] pursuit [noun] of [prep] happiness [noun].

*Probably better termed a 'complementizer.' Like *that*, *for* marks an embedded clause (here, *one people to dissolve the political bands which have conected them with another*).

Chapter Five: Nouns and Verbs: Subclasses and Features

Exercise 1:

paper (mass/count), steel (mass), glue (mass), pen (count), truth (mass; rarely count as in *We hold these truths to be self-evident*), hydrogen (mass), uranium (mass), brick (mass/count), lamp (count), love (mass/ count (count as in *she has many loves*)), muscle (mass/count), stomach (count), typography (mass), spelling (mass; count as in *this spelling of this word*), footnote (count), democracy (mass/count).

Exercise 2:

Proper nouns sometimes do mean more than just their reference. Names which describe qualities of the individual the name refers to--*Fatso, Red,* etc.--are one example of this. Also, a place name like *Antarctica* obviously contains a bound morpheme *ant-* (= *anti-*), meaning 'opposite'; the name was coined to mean the opposite of *Arctic.* And most simply, everyday names for people contain a gender element of meaning. However, proper nouns are semantically different from common noun even when they have these kinds of meanings, because they always denote uniquely one referent in the context of knowledge and assumptions about the world in which they are used.

Exercise 3:

1. All are definite.
2. *A man:* indefinite specific. Others: definite.
3. *You:* indefinite, if the meaning is 'one,' but definite, if the meaning is 'second person.'
    February: definite. *A whale:* indefinite non-specific.
4. Indefinite non-specific.
5. Indefinite specific.

Exercise 4:

1. *see:* 2
2. *hear:* 2
3. *buy:* 3, not just 2, because buying involves a price.
4. *send:* 3
5. *exchange*: 4 (*Jo exchanged the gloves for a hat with Sheila*)
6. *careen:* 2 (*The car careened around the corner*)
7. *imagine:* 2 (the second of which is a proposition, realized most often as a sentence)
8. *listen:* 2
9. *rain:* 0, perhaps surprisingly. The *it* subject of *it rained* is not a true pronoun, since it has no antecedent, and no referent in the world; *rain rained* is not a good paraphrase of *it rained*, an observation which is underscored by non-paraphrases of similar expressions: *it was boring in there* (≠ *boringness was boring*), *it misted all afternoon* (≠ *mist misted*). Rather, *it* here is a "dummy" expression, used only because English has a requirement that every sentence have a subject.
10. *announce:* 3 (the announcer, the announced, and the announcee).

Exercise 5:

The utterance *Paul ate* normally conveys that Paul ate a conventional meal (breakfast, lunch, dinner)--not that he at some unspecified thing. This is different from *Paul ate something,* which conveys that Paul ate some unspecified thing and does not imply that Paul ate a conventional meal. Many, perhaps all, verbs which can occur in both 1- and 2-NP constructions convey the same sort of conventionality, when uttered in the 1-NP version:

> *Max painted* conveys that Max is a painter, or at least that painting is a habitual activity for Max, if only for a short period of time. If A asks what Max did yesterday, and B answers *Max painted,* this implies that for Max, painting is a usual activity.

> *Max baked* conveys that Max is a baker or a person who bakes as a frequent activity. The present writer has baked something no more than five or six times in his life. Given this, it would be strange for someone to say *Jeff Kaplan baked,* even if I spent the whole day baking. (More likely would be *Jeff Kaplan baked a cake (can you believe that?).*)

> *Write* seems to behave as do *paint* and *bake.*

> *Study* appears at first glance slightly different but is really the same. Since so many people study, at some time in their lives, studying may be regarded as a sort of conventional activity which everyone may be expected to engage in. Non-students study (religious texts, contracts, foreign languages at home, etc.) as well as students in regular schools.

> *Read* may be like *study* but more so: Nearly everyone over the age of six reads, so reading is a conventional and usual activity for most people.

> *Drink* conveys something else, at least in many occurrences: *Max drinks* conveys that Max regularly drinks alcoholic beverages, and *Max drank* frequently conveys that Max drank alcohol. (Not always, though: *Exhausted from his trek across the desert, when Max arrived at the oasis and was offered a carafe of cool fresh water, he threw back his head and drank.*)

The examples involving activities that are very common (reading, studying) blur the distinction that is so clear with verbs like *eat.* (Notice that while eating is a common activity (more common, perhaps, than reading or studying), it is conventionally associated with meals, which is just what is conveyed by its 1-NP use.)

Exercise 6:

Causative verbs:

1. *break:* The window broke/We broke the window.
2. *shatter:* The glass shattered/We shattered the glass.
7. *hurt:* My ankle hurts/The brick hurt my ankle.
8. *tickle:* My bee sting tickles/She tickled me.

Exercise 7:

1. Since the identity of the announcer is not only unknown, but also of no importance, the passive is a good choice because it allows omission of the noun expression referring to the announcer--the logical subject.

2. Similarly, since the identity of the heater of the solution is unimportant to the reader (although the identity is known to the writer), the passive is a good choice because it allows omission of the noun expression referring to that individual.

3. In this case, the passive is a good choice for a different reason. The topic is Max. The active counterpart of the given sentence is *Lightning struck Max,* in which the noun *Max* is sentence-final, rather than sentence-initial, the preferred location for topics in sentences with canonical structure. In contrast, the passive sentence puts *Max* in subject--i.e., initial--position.

Exercise 8:

A. First, the *get*-passive occurs primarily in casual contexts. *Jack's house got burned down* is more casual than *Jack's house was burned down.* Second, the *get*- passive is used to convey relatively greater speaker empathy for, or emotional connection with, the referent of the subject. A prototypical case of this connection is when the subject refers to the speaker; thus, *I got run over* is more common than *I was run over* in casual speech. Third, the *get*-passive is common is when the event the sentence describes has salient emotional impact, even if the speaker is not involved. *Jack's house got burned down* is more likely in casual contexts than *Jack's house got painted.*

B. 1. Not passive. The active counterpart--*Someone married Bill and Bonnie*--isn't a good paraphrase of the original sentence.

2. Not passive. No *by*- phrase is possible, at least with Agentive meaning. **Doug got drunk by the bartender* is not possible.

3. Not passive. Trying to construct an active counterpart fails: *Somebody located the Dripping Palms Resort next to a toxic waste dump,* while grammatical, is not a paraphrase of the original. The original does not entail, or even suggest, an Agent (a "doer," here a "locater").

4. Not passive. The sentence entails a state, rather than an event, and cannot have an Agentive *by*- phrase (**My front window is broken by someone*).

Exercise 9:

1. Passive.   2. Active.   3. Middle.   4. Middle.   5. Active.   6. Passive.
7. Active.   8. Active.   9. Passive.   10. Active.

Exercise 10:

The imperative may suggest that the speaker is in a higher status role or a position of greater power than the addressee. It is appropriately uttered by a member of a military organization to a lower-ranking member; the subjunctive does not fit so well in that context. The subjunctive may be more appropriate in a situation where speaker and addressee are of equal status.

Exercise 11:

1. *hear:* stative. *I heard the news from the time it came on until midnight.* (Hence non-instantaneous.) **Al heard the story before I did so. *Al was hearing the news.* (Hence stative.)
2. *listen:* durative. *Al listened to the news for twenty minutes.* (Hence not instantaneous.) *Al listened to the story before I did so. Al was listening to the news.* (Hence not stative.)
3. *amuse:* durative. *Al amused the baby for twenty minutes. Al amused the baby before anyone else could do so. Al was amusing the baby.*
4. *know:* stative. *Maureen knew French for ten years. *Maureen knew French before I did so. *Maureen was knowing French.*
5. *think:* durative. *Sid thought about the problem for ten minutes. Sid thought about the problem before I could do so. Sid was thinking about the problem.*
6. *appoint:* instantaneous. *Humbert appointed Walter secretary at 4 pm. *Humbert appointed Walter secretary from 4 until 6.*
7. *realize:* instantaneous. *At 2 minutes past the hour I realized this was the wrong house. *For the last twelve years I have realized that I would never play for the Yankees.*
8. *receive:* instantaneous. *At seven o'clock I received the telegram.*
9. *explode:* instantaneous. *At ten o'clock the cigar exploded.*
10. *hate:* stative. *Max hated Nixon all his life. *Max hated Nixon not just because Cathy did so. *Max was hating Nixon the whole time he was president.*

Exercise 12:

1. *run:* unbounded: *She will run forever. She will run until she tires.*
2. *drive:* unbounded: *She will drive forever. She will drive until she runs out of gas.*
3. *cross the street:* bounded: **She will cross the street until she tires.* (OK on an interative reading, but bounded on the non-iterative reading.)
4. *win the game:* bounded: **We will win the game all night.*
5. *have a drink:* bounded: **Andy will have a drink until closing time.*
6. *nap:* unbounded: *Sheila will nap until it is time to feed the kittens.*
7. *run a mile:* bounded: **Maury will run a mile forever.*
8. *drive the car:* unbounded: *Maury will drive the car forever.*
9. *read:* unbounded: *He will read until he falls asleep.*
10. *push the cart:* unbounded: *They will push the cart until hell freezes over.*
11. *drink:* unbounded: *He will drink until he runs out of breath.*
12. *build:* bounded: **Bert will build the house in Wyoming until it is done.*

Exercise 13:

1. Tense form: Present. Tense form meaning: futurate (i.e., future time event is planned.) Aspect form and meaning: inherently durative, unbounded.

2. Tense form: Present. Tense form meaning: present time. Aspect form: inherently durative and unbounded; and progressive. Aspect form meaning: event in progress at time referred to by tense form.

3. Tense form: Past. Tense form meaning: hypothetical event. Aspect form: inherently durative, bounded; iterative.

4. Tense form: Present. Tense form meaning: "timeless truth." Aspect form and meaning: inherently durative, bounded; iterative.

5. Tense form: Present. Tense form meaning: present time reference for a "performative" use of the verb. Aspect form and meaning: inherently instantaneous.

6. Tense form: Future. Tense form meaning: probability in the present. Aspect form and meaning: inherently stative; unbounded.

7. Tense form: present. Tense form meaning: present time, with the implication that the state denoted by the verb extends forward and backward from the time of speaking. Aspect form and meaning: stative.

Exercise 14:

1. Hot News.   2. Existential.   3. Resultative.   4. Continuative.   5. Existential.
6. Existential (or perhaps Hot News).   7. Hot News.   8. Continuative.

Additional Exercise:

The rabbit-hole: noun phrase, definite, containing a count noun *rabbit-hole,* itself a compound.

a tunnel: noun phrase, indefinite, nonspecific, containing a count noun *tunnel.*

dipped: verb, past tense referring to past time, instantaneous aspect.

Alice: proper noun.

herself: feminine reflexive pronoun (antecedent: *Alice*).

she: third person singular feminine pronoun (antecedent: *Alice*), feminine, subject case form.

found: verb, past tense indicating past time, instantaneous aspect.

fell: verb, past tense indicating past time, durative, unbounded aspect.

her: third person singular feminine pronoun (antecedent: *she*), object case form.

was coming: past tense (referring to past time) form of *be coming,* i.e., of *be...-ing* and *come; be...-ing* marking progressive aspect.

noticed: past tense verb, indicating past time; instantaneous aspect.

maps: noun, plural, count.

truths: a mass noun here used as a count noun, plural.

are endowed by: passive construction. Present tense form, for timeless truth. Inherently instantaneous aspect with a stative interpretation deriving from the "timeless truth" sense of the present tense form. Plural verb *are* agreeing in number with subject noun phrase *they.*

liberty: mass, abstract noun.

to secure: infinitive verb construction.

deriving: present participle, with verbal function.

powers: mass noun here used as a count noun, plural.

Chapter 6: Phrase Structure

Exercise 1:

A. 1. *over the mountain:* The bear went <u>there</u>.
    2. *the mountain:* The bear went over <u>it</u>.

B. 1. She put a <u>red</u> apple in the barrel.
    2. Ask <u>Gina</u> for some more pie.
    3. <u>George</u> can handle multi-tasking.
    4. A <u>kitten</u> raced around the paddock.
    5. Attila believed <u>Henry</u>.

C. 1.   *Try to <u>show</u> fortieth president could read.
         *Try to <u>this</u> fortieth president could read.
         *Try to <u>deny</u> fortieth president could read.

    2.   *For best <u>production</u> Sears staples in the right size for each job.
         *For best <u>business</u> Sears staples in the right size for each job.

    3.   *Marino dropped back <u>but</u> a spiral to the receiver.
         *Marino dropped back <u>sent</u> a spiral to the receiver.
         *Marino dropped back <u>this</u> a spiral to the receiver.

    4.   *The Secretary announced that the <u>prisoners</u>.
         *The Secretary announed that the <u>freedom</u>.

Exercise 2:

A. All can be justified by substitution:

    (a) Max bought <u>balls</u> for <u>Jane</u>
    (c) <u>Sam</u> burned <u>leaves</u>
    (e) <u>George</u> was surprising to no one
    (g) She said he would wash the dishes, and he did <u>this</u>

B. 1.   It would not be wise [for Smith to fire Wesson]
    2.   [When her keeper came], Hippy the hippo roared with laughter
    3.   [Fast closer] though Flicka was, she didn't win all her races.

Exercise 3:

1. [A large python] and [a small octopus] curled around Sharon's leg.
2. Max believed [that the moon was made of green cheese] and [that Mars was covered by a web of canals].
3. John is [taking it with him] and [putting it into the convertible].
4. A [little child] and [friendly puppy] shall lead them.
5. Mannie and Mo [tried to convince Jack to resign] and [sent a letter to that effect to headquarters].

Exercise 4:

1. Greg and Steve [built a mountain house]. They <u>did so</u> in order to live in peace.
2. I doubt [tomorrow will be sunny]. But the weatherman really believes <u>it</u>.
3. [Automobile companies] resist attempts by consumer groups to get <u>them</u> to recall vehicles for safety reasons.
4. Put the tinsel [on the tree], not under it; and put it <u>there</u> because that's where it belongs.

Exercise 5:

A.

1.

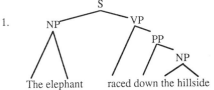

2.

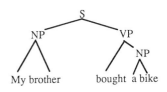

3.

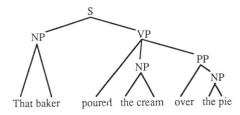

B.

(1) [NP [Det My] [N brother]] [VP [VP [V bought] [NP [[Det a] [N car]]] [PP [P for] [NP [N $2,000]]]]]

(2) [NP [NP [Art The] [N skater]] [S [[NP [Pro who]] [VP [V fell] [PP [P on] [NP [Art the] [N ice]]]]]]] [VP [M-Adv quickly] [VP [V jumped] [P up]]]

31

Exercise 6:

A.

1.

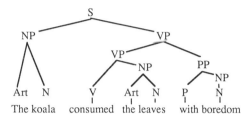

2.

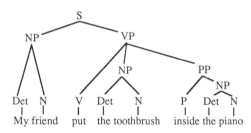

3.

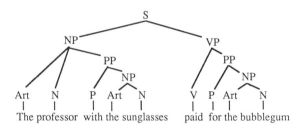

4.

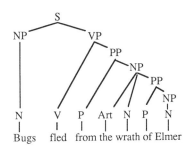

B.

1.   I don't like hot chili and hot curry.   I don't like chili that is hot, and curry.

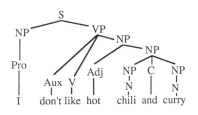   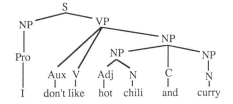

2.   I love to visit in-laws.   I love in-laws who are visiting.

3.   Popeye loved Olive more than Bluto did.   Popeye loved Olive more than he loved Bluto.

4.   I decided to choose the truck.   I decided while on the truck.

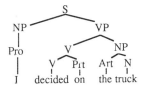   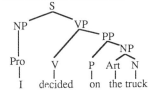

33

5.　　　They found the treasure which was　　　Under the stairs, they found the treasure
　　　 under the stairs

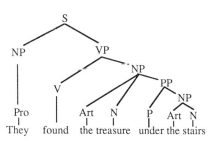
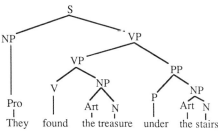

They found the treasure under the stairs　　　They found the treasure under the stairs

6.　　　The young ones are ready to be eaten　　　The young ones are ready to eat something

Exercise 7:

1.　　*James Michener's long novels* is a constituent, an NP, so it can be shared; therefore, the sentence is fine.

2.　　*Sincere and sweet* is a constituent, an adjective phrase (composed of a conjoined pair of adjectives), so the sentence is grammatical.

3.　　*Little poems to all the nieces and nephews* is not a constituent, and neither are *Uncle Lew wrote* or *Aunt Bonnie delivered,* so the sentence is bad.

4.　　*The effects of layoffs on faculty morale* is a constituent, an NP, so the sentence is fine.

5.　　Because *up* is a particle, not a preposition, it forms a constituent with the preceding verb. Consequently neither *up the deans* nor *up the department chairs* is a constituent. Since *Day called* is not a constituent either, the sentence has neither a conjunction of constituents nor a sharing of a constituent; as a result, it is ungrammatical.

6.　　*Quite appropriately and efficiently* is a constitutent, an Adverb Phrase, so it can be shared; as a result, the sentence is fine.

7.　　*The company to stop polluting the river* is not a constituent, and neither is *Fetzer thought he had persuaded* or *Karpov really forced,* so the sentence is bad.

Exercise 8:

1. teacher.　　2. guy.　　3. Anyone.　　4. riddle.　　5. types.　　6. person.　　7. man.

Exercise 9:

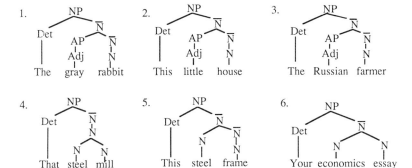

Comments: (4) contains a compound noun, *steel mill*. (5) doesn't; it has, rather, an attributive modifier noun, *steel*. In (5), *steel* functions rather like an adjective; in (4) *steel* functions more like a direct object noun expression (the mill 'mills steel.'). (6) is like (4) in that *economics* has a direct object-like relation to the noun *essay*. (It's an 'essay on economics.') Notice that wherever there is an N̄, *one*-pronominalization is possible, with the exception of (6), which is presumably due to a quirk in the grammar of possessive determiners; and wherever there is just an N, *one*-pronominalization is not possible.

Exercise 10:

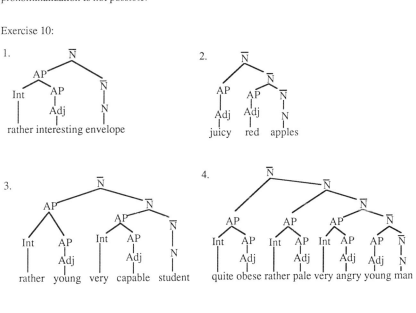

35

Exercise 11:

1.

Evidence: the borrower of the scary *one;*
*the *one* of the scary mystery.

2.

Evidence: the borrower with a [short] crewcut;
the *one* with a crewcut.

3.

Evidence: the student of literature with a [red]
ponytail; *the *one* of literature...; the *one*
with a ponytail.

4.

Evidence: the *one* with a ponytail;
the student with a [long] ponytail.

Exercise 12:

1.

2.

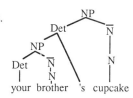

3.

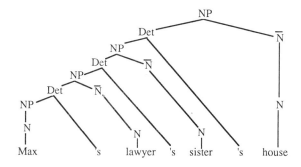

Exercise 13:

1.

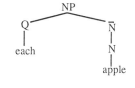

2.

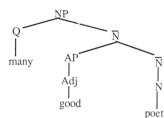

3.

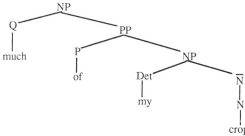

4.

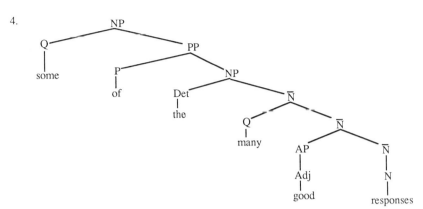

Exercise 14:

A.

1.

2.

3.

4.

5.

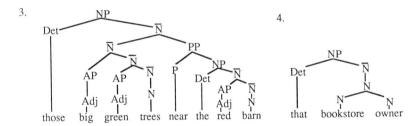

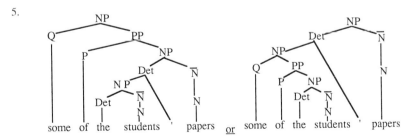

B.

1.

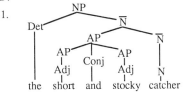

2.

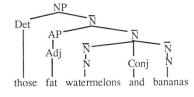

3.

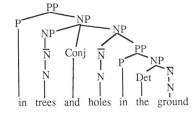

4.

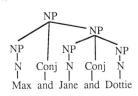
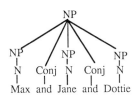

C.   In the examples in which *one* cannot refer back to a final noun in a noun string, the preceding word or words in the noun string bear a closer type of relation to the final noun than in the examples in which *one* can refer back to a final noun. This relation, the "complement" relation, is akin to the relation a direct object noun expression bears to a verb. So, in (1), *bookstore owner,* the noun *bookstore* is a complement of *owner,* just as, in the verb expression *owns a bookstore,* the expression *a bookstore* is the direct object of *owns.* Similarly, in (2), *textbook author, textbook* is the complement of *author,* and *author* functions rather like a verb (cf. *he authored a textbook*). The same kind of relation can be found in (3), *lakefront property developer,* and (4), *Russian teacher.* In contrast, in the examples in which *one* can refer back to a final noun in a noun string, the relation between the final noun and preceding words in the string is an "attribute" relation, a relation rather

39

like that borne by an adjective to the noun it modifies. Notice that in none of the examples (5) - (9) would it make sense to say that the non-final material in the noun string functions like a direct object of the last noun in the string.

Exercise 15:

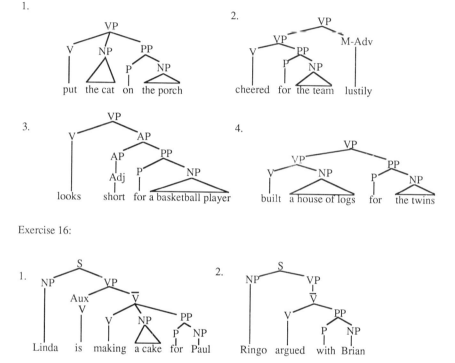

Exercise 16:

5.

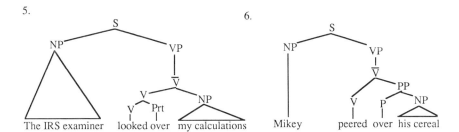

6.

7.

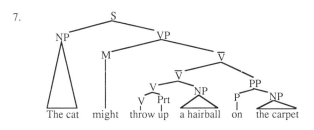

8.

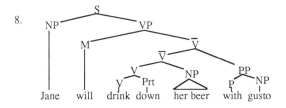

Exercise 17:

Trees shown with progressively less detail:

1.

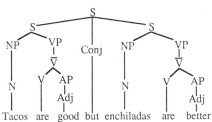

41

2.

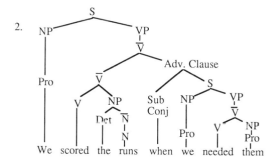

3.

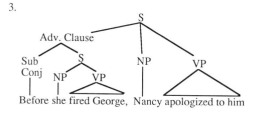

4.

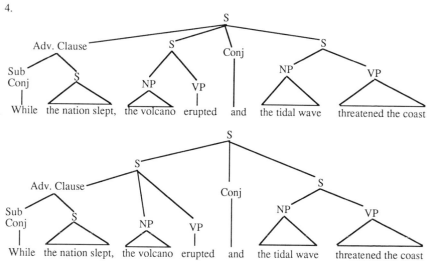

These two trees represent different meanings of the ambiguous sentence. Note: an alternative to the first tree would be one with the following structure:

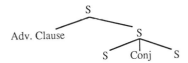

Exercise 18:

A.   Trees in progressively less detail:

1.

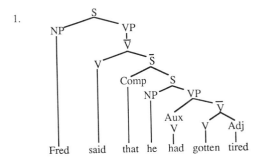

Fred   said   that   he   had   gotten   tired

2.

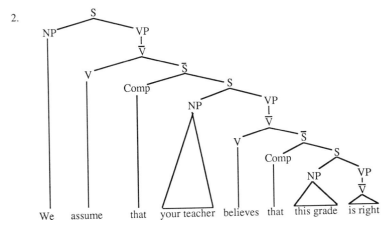

We   assume   that   your teacher   believes   that   this grade   is right

43

3.

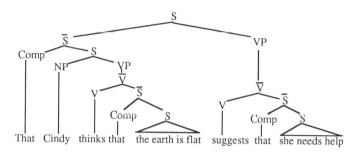

That Cindy thinks that the earth is flat suggests that she needs help

4.

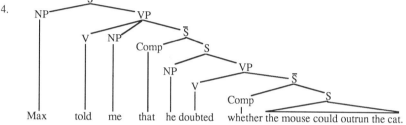

Max told me that he doubted whether the mouse could outrun the cat.

B.   Since these examples contain conjunctions of NPs and S̄s but are ungrammatical, they
support the hypothesis that S̄s are not NPs.

Exercise 19:

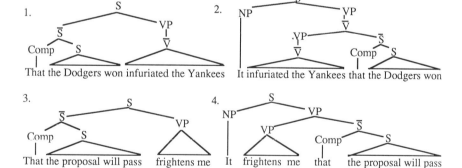

1.
That the Dodgers won infuriated the Yankees

2.
It infuriated the Yankees that the Dodgers won

3.
That the proposal will pass frightens me

4.
It frightens me that the proposal will pass

5.

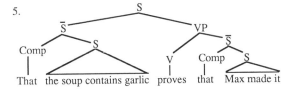

That the soup contains garlic proves that Max made it

6.

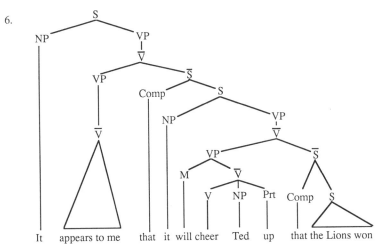

It appears to me that it will cheer Ted up that the Lions won

Exercise 20:

1.

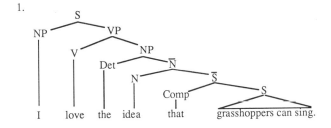

I love the idea that grasshoppers can sing.

2.

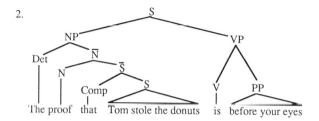

3.

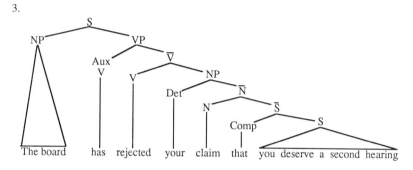

4.

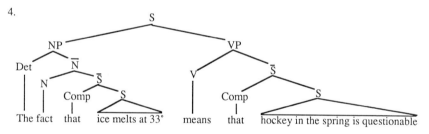

Exercise 21:

A.

1.

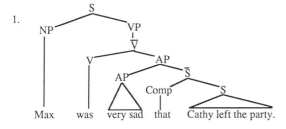

2.

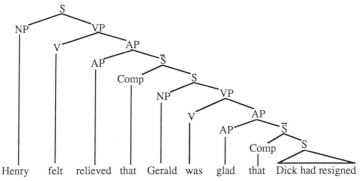

3.

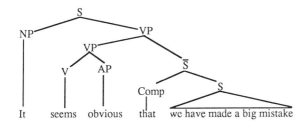

B. *Happy, sad, pleased, excited,* but not *red, tall, shiny,* etc., encode attitudes which
individuals can have toward propositions. Other such adjectives include *delighted, afraid,
worried, sure, confident,* and *mistaken.* These adjectives relate entities capable of having a
psychological attitude toward a proposition--basically, human beings--and those
propositions. Adjectives which cannot take propositonal complements include *big, small,
round, smooth, sweet, striped, fat, dead, wooden, folded, visual,* and *loud.* Another
class of adjectives which can take complement clauses includes, among others, *significant,
important, unlucky, good, obvious,* and *troublesome.* When adjectives of the latter type
take complement clauses, they do so in extraposition structures--*It is significant that S,*

etc., and in forms with sentential subjects--*That S is significant,* etc., rather than as predicates relating entities capable of psychological reactions to propositions and those propositions.

Exercise 22:

1.

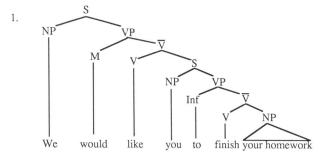

2.

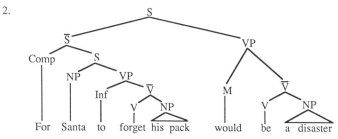

3.

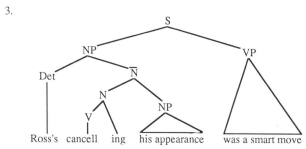

Chapter Seven.   Grammatical Relations and Semantic Roles

Exercise 1:

Topics of sentences:

S1: rain.
S2: probably: a game at Pittsburgh.
S3: the game.
S4: the game's being called.
S5: this (the game's being called quickly).
S6: an official protest.
S7: a game being called in less than 45 minutes.
S8: the game? the game's being called (quickly)? something [the speaker] had coming?

Exercise 2:

1.   [The boys]: Agent. [the glass]: Patient. [a stone]: Instrument.
2.   [The ice]: Patient.
3.   [Steve]: Patient or Experiencer. [Newton Corner]: Locative.
4.   [Mary Ellen]: Experiencer.
5.   [Peter]: Agent. [a new Chevy]: Patient. [Mary Ellen]: Recipient or "Benefactive," a role
     not listed. (The "Benefactive" role would apply to Mary Ellen in the situation in which
     Peter didn't buy her the new Chevy, but performed the buying for her, as her
     representative).
6.   [The kids]: Agent, Experiencer, or even Patient. [the door]: Source.
7.   [Charlie]: Experiencer. [Hallie]: Patient.
8.   [Greg]: Experiencer. [the weather in Chicago]: Patient.
9.   [God]: Agent. [the heavens and the earth]: Effected.

Exercise 3:

phone: A, R.   catch: A, P.   own: R? (or E?), P.   blush: P.   hand: A, P, R.
admire: E, P.   sit: A, Loc.   have: R? (E?), P.   sell: A, R, P, "Amount."
hurry: A.

Exercise 4:

read: A, P   design: A, P   have: E (or R? or P?), P   open: (A) (I), P

$\left(\begin{smallmatrix} \Downarrow \\ \varnothing \end{smallmatrix}\right)$

break: (A,) (I,) P   plant: A, P   pinch: A, (I,) $\left\{\begin{smallmatrix} E \\ P \end{smallmatrix}\right\}$ dissolve: P (Loc)

paint: A, P   add: $\left\{\begin{smallmatrix} A \\ I \end{smallmatrix}\right\}$ P, "Ground"   reflect: (A,) (I,) P, (Destination)

Examples: *pinch:* John (A) pinched Mary (E) (with a clothes pin (I)); The clothes pin (I)
pinched Mary (E); John (A) pinched the sleeve (P). *dissolve:* The sugar (P) dissolved (in

the water (Loc)). The water (Loc) dissolved the sugar (P). *add:* John (A) added 2 (P) to 16 (Ground). John (A) added 2 (P) and 16 (Ground). This article (I) adds much (P) to our understanding (Ground). The author (A) adds much (P) to our understanding (Ground) with his analysis (I). *reflect:* John (A) used a mirror (I) to reflect light (P) into the window (Destination). The mirror (I) reflected light (P) into Max's eyes (Destination). The smooth surface (I) reflected the light (P). The light (P) reflected.

Exercise 5:

1. *Glen and Molly:* verb agreement: this NP is plural, and the agreeing verb, *love,* is plural in agreement. Tag-formation: this NP gets copied to form a tag: *Glen and Molly love cheesecake, don't they?*

2. *The auditor:* verb agreement: *loves;* tag formation: *...doesn't he?*

3. *The jury:* verb agreement: *has;* tag: *has it?*

4. *It:* verb agreement: *is;* tag: *isn't it?*

5. *Yesterday:* verb agreement: *was;* tag: *wasn't it?*

6. *The lawyer in charge:* verb agreement: *was;* tag: An interesting conflict arises between the sexist expectation in our culture that lawyers will be men, and the gender of the lawyer mentioned in this sentence. For many speakers, no tag question can be legitimately formed from this sentence, all of the following sounding a bit odd:

   a) ?The lawyer in charge was Mary Ann, wasn't he?
   b) ?The lawyer in charge was Mary Ann, wasn't she?
   c) ?The lawyer in charge was Mary Ann, wasn't it?

   --whereas *The lawyer in charge was Tom, wasn't he?* doesn't sound odd at all.

Exercise 6:

1. Actual (superficial): *Marie.* Logical: *the people.*
2. Actual: *The ball.* Logical: *the lunging fielder.*
3. Actual: *The announcement.* Logical: unspecified *(someone).*
4. Actual: *A hundred dollars.* Logical: *her aunt.*
5. Actual: *Book authors.* Logical: *the indexing problem.*
6. Actual: None. Logical: *You.*
7. Actual: *Senator Crookshark.* Logical: unspecified (not *someone,* since groups or institutions indict, not individuals).
8. Actual: *There.* Logical: *the police.*

Exercise 7:

1. *the pencil.*
2. *John.*
3. none.
4. *this table.*
5. *oregano, sage, curry, butter, garlic, and onions.*

6.   none.
7.   *me.*
8.   *the oasis.*
9.   *the courtroom.*
10.   *the hall.*
11.   none.
12.   none.
13.   none; but something like a direct object function is manifested by *this plane,* because of the passive *This plane was flown in by George Bush.* This passive is made possible by a "reanalysis" of *fly in* as a verb, instead of as a verb + preposition. (Some speakers will find this example unacceptable; others will accept it in casual contexts; still others will find it fully acceptable.)
14.   *that Ronnie fell asleep in cabinet meetings.*
15.   If passivizability and post-verb position defines direct object, then *the company* functions as direct object. But see Chapter Eight (p. 331-334) for discussion.

Exercise 8:

1.   *the cub scouts:* surface Indirect Object (IO), as well as underlying IO.
2.   No IO.
3.   *my invalid aunt:* underlying IO, but surface Direct Object (DO). Underlying form: *I wrote a long letter to my invalid aunt yesterday.* In the surface form of the sentence, *my invalid aunt* is in post-verb position and is passivizable, making it a DO (*My invalid aunt was written a letter...*).
4.   *Celia:* underlying IO, but surface DO. Same analysis as for no. 3.
5.   No IO. (Arguably there is an underlying IO *me.*)
6.   *me:* surface and underlying IO.
7.   No IO.
8.   *me:* surface DO (it's passivizable: *I was charged a lot by that mechanic...*). Is it an underlying IO? Maybe. To call it an underlying IO requires positing underlying forms that are ungrammatical: *That mechanic charged a lot to me to tune up my lawnmower,* which is a theoretical cost.

Additional exercises:

B.

1.   [The trailer]: subject.
2.   [Those students]: subject. [cookies]: direct object. [the dean]: indirect object and object of a preposition.
3.   [Wesson]: direct object (note that it is passivizable) under this chapter's analysis, but see Chapter Eight. [a bore]: object complement.
4.   [Sandra]: direct object. [a new beach house]: none (at the surface level).
5.   [Early poets]: subject. [the effect of sports on humans]: direct object.
6.   [Linguistics]: subject. [the scientific study of language]: predicate nominative.
7.   [Seven old ladies]: subject. [the lavatory]: object of a preposition.
8.   [The bone]: subject. [Rover]: object of a preposition.
9.   [Alice]: subject. [her sister]: object of a preposition. [the bank]: object of a preposition. [the book her sister was reading]: object of a preposition. [her sister]: subject. [no pictures]: none. [the use of a book]: none. [Alice]: subject.

Chapter Eight: Noncanonical Sentence Forms

Exercise 1:

1. Focussed phrase (FP): *the onions.* Assumed background proposition (ABP): *Something ruined the stew.*
2. FP: *Sally.* ABP: *Someone called you.*
3. FP: *Bill's cat.* ABP. *Something bit the mail carrier.*
4. FP: *smoke pot in class.* ABP: *Mary does something.*
5. FP: *washing last night's dishes in the morning.* ABP: *I really hate something.*

Exercise 2:

1. You can pass the salt =>(subject-aux inversion) Can you pass the salt?

2. A person should answer a question with a question =>(*not-* insertion) A person should not answer a question with a question =>(subject-aux inversion) Should a person not answer a question with a question?

3. Max has bothered the principal enough =>(*not-* insertion) Max has not bothered the principal enough =>(contraction) Max hasn't bothered the principal enough =>(subject-aux inversion) Hasn't Max bothered the principal enough?

4. You like 0 garbanzo beans =>(subject-aux inversion) 0 like garbanzo beans =>(*do-* insertion) Do 0 you like garbanzo beans? (NOTE: The "0" is the allomorph of the present tense morpheme which occurs in persons and numbers other than third person singular.)

5. You hate 0 violent movies =>(*not-* insertion) You not hate 0 violent movies =>(tense-shifting) You 0 not hate violent movies =>(contraction) You 0n't hate violent movies =>(subject-aux inversion) 0n't you hate violent movies =>(*do-* insertion) don't you hate violent movies.

    (NOTE: Alternative orders are possible. For example, *do-* insertion might immediately follow tense-shifting, so the *not* could attach to the *do* rather than to the unattached tense suffix. The earliest transformational treatment of the phenomena of tense location and question formation (which is still considered quite elegant and which the description in this chapter does some violence to) appeared in Noam Chomsky's classic *Syntactic Structures* (The Hague: Mouton, 1957).

Exercise 3:

A and B together:

1. I should hand what to Sam =>(subject-aux inversion) Should I hand what to Sam =>(*wh-* fronting) What should I hand to Sam?

2. We can visit Sam where =>(subject-aux inversion) Can we visit Sam where =>(*wh-* fronting) Where can we visit Sam?

3. You said (i.e., *say -ed*) what to Sam =>(subject-"aux" inversion) -ed you say what to Sam

=>(*do-* insertion) did you say what to Sam =>(*wh-* fronting) What did you say to Sam?

4. You exchanged what for the socks =>(subject-"aux" inversion) -ed you exchange what for the socks =>(*do-* insertion) did you exchange what for the socks =>(*wh-* fronting) What did you exchange for the socks?

5. Who will come to Sam's party =>(subject-aux inversion) will who come to Sam's party =>(*wh-* fronting) Who will come to Sam's party?

Exercise 4:

1. Some of the students will leave =>(pro and aux copy) Some of the students will leave they will =>(*not-* insertion) Some of the students will leave they will not =>(contraction) Some of the students will leave they won't => (subject-aux inversion) Some of the students will leave won't they?

2. My sister shouldn't stay =>(pro and aux copy) My sister shouldn't stay she should =>(subject-aux inversion) My sister shouldn't stay should she?

3. I am the chair of this committee =>(pro and aux copy) I am the chair of this committee I am =>(*not-* insertion) I am the chair of this committee I am not =>(subject-aux inversion) I am the chair of this committee am I not?

4. This computer has been checked out =>(pro and aux copy) This computer has been checked out it has =>(*not-* insertion) This computer has been checked out it has not =>(contraction) This computer has been checked out it hasn't =>(subject-aux inversion) This computer has been checked out hasn't it?

Exercise 5:

A. The plain imperative is more peremptory, better suited to a context in which the speaker has a higher status than the addressee and in addition has a social relationship with the addressee enabling the speaker to issue commands to the addressee. This applies to imperatives that function as commands, not to those that function as invitations, suggestions, or advice. The tagged imperative is more appropriate to interaction between equals or to situations in which the speaker does not have a role enabling the speaker to issue commands to the addressee.

B. (i)   The speaker assumes nothing about the state of the door.
    (ii) The speaker assumes that the door is open, but that assumption has been called into question.
    (iii) The speaker assumes that the door is open, but that assumption has been called into question. A speaker of (iii) may have more confidence in this assumption than the speaker of (ii).
    (iv) The speaker assumes that the door is not open.

Exercise 6:

B: These examples indicate that not all inversions have non-inverted paraphrases, since none of these examples do: *Israel and El Salvador and the six eastern Caribbean nations allied with the operation...were joining the U.S. in opposing the resolution.; *A mosaic of four *fruit sauces is surrounding the creation.; *A body of men in blue rode coming up the street..*

Exercise 7:

To answer this question, these examples must be changed into canonical forms. Then it is easy to see what kind of *be* a sentence contains.

1. 20 men *were* on the deck: main verb.
2. 20 men may have *been* parading in front of us: aux (progressive).
3. Seven players will *be* released by the Packers today: aux (of passive).
4. *Some problems might *be* with that analysis: main verb.
5. *Somebody should have *been* to meet me at the train: main verb. (Cf. *there is somebody at the train.*)
6. Somebody should have *been* appointed to meet me at the train: aux (passive).
7. Some flies *are* swimming happily in my chowder: aux (progressive).

Conclusion: it doesn't matter whether the *be* is an aux or a main verb. Either kind can occur with existential *there*.

Exercise 8:

NP   (Aux) *be* X => There (Aux) *be*   NP   X.
[-def]   [-def]

I.e., an indefinite NP followed optionally by an aux and a form of *be* may be transformed into a structure beginning with *there*, followed by the optional aux and the form of *be* and the 'moved' NP. The 'X' is a variable, standing for anything. It often contains a locative (*There is a fly in my soup*). It can be null (*There is a God*). The point of examples (2) and (3) is that the subject NP cannot be definite. The point of examples (4) and (5) is that the verb must be *be*. The formulation of the transformation lets *be* be either an aux or a main verb.

Exercise 9:

1.

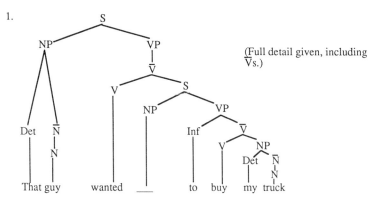

(Full detail given, including V̄s.)

2.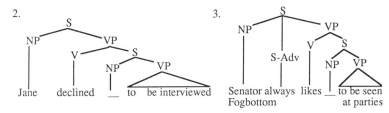

3.

4.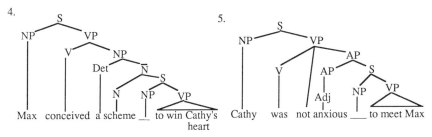

5.

Comment on no. 4: The empty NP, meaning 'Max,' is subject of an embedded S that is the complement of the noun *scheme*, rather than of a sequence *conceived a scheme*. The reason is that *a scheme to win Cathy's heart* is a constituent, as can be seen from the passive *A scheme to win Cathy's heart was conceived by Max.*

Exercise 10:

A.

1.	like *persuade*. The post-verb material cannot be *wh*- clefted: *What the cop forced was for Sheila to pull over.*

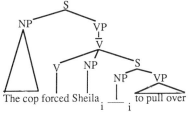

2.   like *persuade*. The post-verb material cannot be *wh*- clefted: *What Ernie begged was for Bert to give back his hat.*

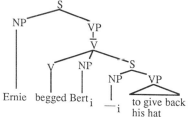

3.   Like *want*. The post-verb material can be *wh*- clefted: *What Terry likes is for Mary Ellen to read to him.* No gap.

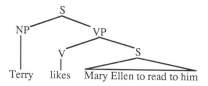

4.   Like *want*. The post-verb material can be *wh*- clefted: *What Tony hated was for his guests to arrive early*.

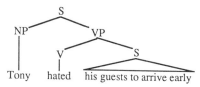

B.   *Promise* is like neither *want* nor *persuade*. The structure of a *promise* sentence is like this:

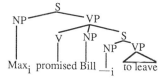

In this structure, the antecedent for the gap is the subject NP, as is the case in *want* sentences; but, unlike *want* sentences, there is a direct object NP in the "upstairs" sentence. The reason is that the sequence *Bill to leave* is not a constituent: it cannot be *wh*- clefted: *What Max promised was for Bill to leave.* Rather, the sequence __*to leave* is cleftable: *Whata Max promised Bill was to leave.*

Exercise 11:

Clefting: *What everybody believed was for Ron to be lying. Indicates that the sequence Ron to be lying is not a constituent. This test suggests that believe sentences may be like sentences with persuade, not expect, i.e., with the structure ...[$_{VP}$ believe NP$_i$] [$_S$ __$_i$ to $\bar{V}$].

Subject-only NPs: Everybody believed it to be raining, ...believed there to be a problem, ...believed the cat to be out of the bag. Indicates that the the post-verb NP is a 'downstairs' subject, not an 'upstairs' direct object. This suggests that believe sentences are like expect, with the structure ...believe [$_S$ NP to $\bar{V}$].

Though- preposing: Though they will believe the senator to have baked the cookies, the reporters will probably ask where he got them anyway => *Believe the reporters though they will to have baked the cookies, the reporters will probably ask where he got them anyway. Since the sequence believe the reporters is not preposable, it must not be a constituent. Under this test, believe behaves just the way expect does.

Passive: Everybody believed the senator to have lied => *For the senator to have lied was believed by everybody. This test indicates that the sequence the senator to have lied is not a constituent. If believe sentences have a persuade- type structure, that sequence is not a constituent. So the result of this test indicates that believe sentences are structured like persuade sentences.

Summary of tests: The clefting and passive tests indicate that believe sentences are not structured like expect sentences. But the tests based on NPs which can only be subjects and on though-preposing indicate that believe sentences are structured like expect sentences. A possible resolution to this conflict of evidence is to hypothesize that expect sentences contain an embedded sentence that is an $\bar{S}$, not an S. Since an $\bar{S}$ contains a complementizer, this would account for the clefting possibility, since the cleft sentence always contains the complementizer for. On the other hand, since no cleft is possible for a believe sentence, a believe sentence, according to this hypothesis, is just an S, not an $\bar{S}$. The hypothesis that believe and expect differ in the type of embedded clauses they contain can be extended to the sub-hypothesis that when a clause is passivized, it is always an $\bar{S}$, never just an S, that is subject to passivization. Independent evidence to support this comes from that- clause passives, which are possible with both expect and believe: That the reporters were getting close to the answer was expected/believed by many of the senators. So believe may take two kinds of clausal complements: $\bar{S}$, with the complementizer that, and S, with (of course) no complementizer. Expect takes only $\bar{S}$ complements, with the complementizer that (and a tensed clause) or with the complementizer for (and an infinitival clause). (Either way, the complementizers can be omitted: We expected (that) he would leave, We believed (that) he would leave.)

Exercise 12:

1.   2.

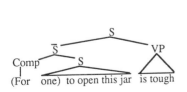

57

3.

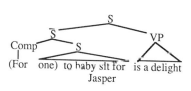

4.

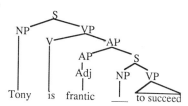

5.

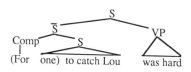

Exercise 13:

A.

1. Underlying structure: Superficial structure:

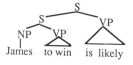   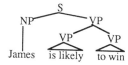

2. Underlying structure: Superficial structure:

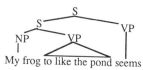   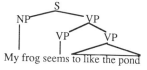

3. Underlying structure: Superficial structure:

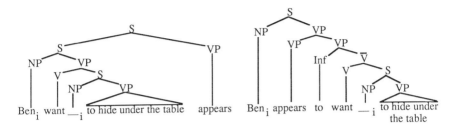

B. *turn out* and *be certain:* The arguments that worked for *seem*, etc., apply unchanged. Both take idiom chunk subjects: *The cat turned out to be out of the bag, The cat is certain to be out of the bag.* They can both take existential *there: There turned out to be a problem, There is certain to be a problem.* And they can both take weather *it: It turned out to be raining, It was certain to rain.*

C. *Happen* and *begin* are also like *seem,* etc. They both take idiom chunk subjects: *The cat happened to be out of the bag, The fur began to fly.* They take existential *there: There happened to be a crowd in the plaza, There began to be some concern.* And they both take weather *it: It happened to be raining, It began to rain.*

Exercise 14:

1.

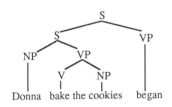

2.

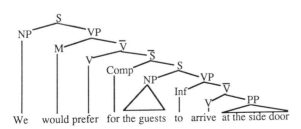

3.

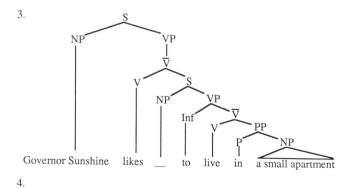

Governor Sunshine likes __ to live in a small apartment

4.

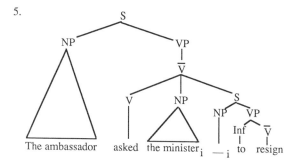

She believed him to be deceiving her

5.

The ambassador asked the minister$_i$ —$_i$ to resign

6.

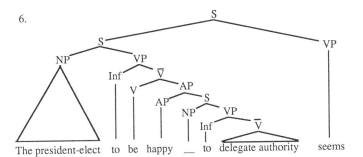

The president-elect   to be   happy   __   to   delegate authority   seems

7.

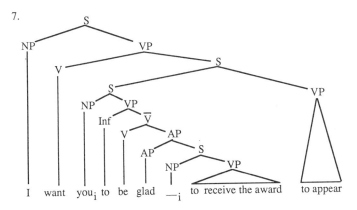

I   want   you$_i$ to   be   glad   __$_i$ to receive the award   to appear

8.

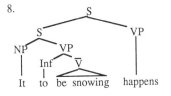

It   to   be   snowing   happens

9.

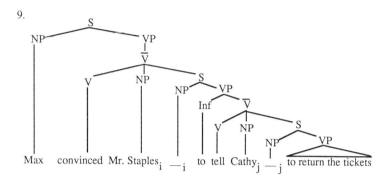

Max   convinced   Mr. Staples$_i$ —$_i$ to tell   Cathy$_j$ —$_j$ to return the tickets

10.

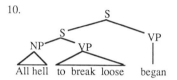

All hell   to break   loose   began

Exercise 15:

1. Max's loving Cathy surprised Peter.
2. The students were surprised at the principal's not being here.
3. Keeping one's lawn mowed can keep neighbors off one's doorstep.
4. Jogging is healthful.
5. The manager's not warning Tom not to pitch to Jack will long be remembered.
6. The turkey's being basted too often was responsible for its greasiness.

Exercisse 16:

hope: takes infinitive complement, not a gerund complement (*I hope to win, *I hope winning*).
Fits Bolinger's suggestion, since what one hopes for is in the future or is unrealized from the perspective of the hoper (one can hope that something has happened, but not if one knows that it has).

risk: takes gerund, not infinitive, complement (*She risked traveling to Miami, *She risked to travel to Miami*). Fits Bolinger's suggestion, since at the time one risks something, the something is realized. A gambler only risks money when the chips are on the table.

start: takes both infinitive and gerund complements (*They started smoking, they started to smoke*). Intuitions may differ as to whether the two complement types encode slightly different meanings. Many native speakers of English may feel there is no difference at all.

continue: takes both (*They continued drinking, they continued to drink*). No clear difference in meaning.

admit: takes gerund, not infinitive, complement (*He admitted robbing the bank, *he admitted to have robbed the bank*). Fits Bolinger's suggestion, since what is admitted is a past event or present state, both "real."

refuse: takes infinitive, not gerund, complement (*We refused to leave, *We refused leaving*). What one refuses to do is a contemplated act in the future, hence 'unrealized.'

plan: When the subject of the embedded clause is the same as the subject of the main clause, it is, of course, 'understood'; in that case only the infinitive occurs (*She planned to leave, *She planned leaving*). This fits with Bolinger's suggestion, since what one plans must be a future act. But when the subject of the embedded clause is different from the subject of the main clause, it must be overt, and in that case both infinitive and gerund can occur (*She planned John's leaving the company, she planned for John to leave the company*). The meaning difference between these two examples is predictable from Bolinger's suggestion: *she planned John's leaving the company* implies not just planning that the event will occur, but planning how it will occur, which comprehends more control by the referent of the main sentence subject than is the case in the situation described by *she planned for John to leave the company,* which implies merely planning that the event will occur, not the details of its unfolding.

Exercise 17:

1. *believe:* nonfactive: *She believed that Cary had baked the cookies* does not presuppose that Cary baked the cookies, as can be seen from the negative form S*he did not believe that Cary had baked the cookies,* which does not entail that Cary baked the cookies.

    note: factive: *The reporters noted that the President had left the room* presupposes that the President had left the room, as can be seen from the negative form *The reporters did not note that the President had left the room,* which entails that the President had left the room.

    be astonishing: factive: *It is astonishing that Tegucigalpa is the capital of Bulgaria* presupposes that Tegucigalpa is the capital of Bulgaria, as can be seen from the negative form *It is not astonishing that Tegucigalpa is the capital of Bulgaria,* which entails that Tegucigalpa is the capital of Bulgaria.

    bother: factive: *It bothers Jane that Saskatoon is the capital of Prince Edward Island* presupposes that Saskatoon is the capital of P.E.I, as can be seen from the negative form *It doesn't bother Jane that Saskatoon is the capital of P.E.I.,* which entails that Saskatoon is the capital of P.E.I.

    doubt: nonfactive: *The reporters doubt that Prof. Conroy actually has the file* does not presuppose that Prof. C. has the file.

    be unfortunate: factive: *That Ned wrote a mystery about computers is unfortunate* presupposes that Ned wrote a mystery about computers, as can be seen from the negative form *That Ned wrote a mystery about computers is not unfortunate,* which entails that Ned wrote a mystery about computers.

2. *believe:* Generally, this nonfactive verb cannot take a gerund clause (**John believed Mary's stealing the silver*), but can take an infinitive clause (*John believed Mary to hve stolen the silver*). Bolinger's principle might predict the opposite, since one can believe something about the past or the present, more 'real' than the future. It might be supposed that the uncertainty of belief as opposed to knowledge is behind the co-occurrence pattern,

but *know* also occurs with infinitives, but not gerunds (*John knew Mary to have stolen the silver,* **John knew Mary's stealing the silver*).

But there is a use of *believe* with gerund clauses. Consider *Did you believe Bill's scoring 40 points last night? I couldn't believe it.* This exemplifies a use which occurs when the context provides the presupposition that the content of the complement clause is true (rather than coming from the factivity of main verb). This use fits with Bolinger's principle, as does *believe* 's being nonfactive.

note: this factive verb takes a gerund clause (*We noted the senator's leaving early*), but not an infinitive clause (**We noted the senator to have left early*). Predictable from Bolinger's principle, since we can note a fact about the present or past, something relatively 'real.'

be astonishing: this factive adjective expression takes both gerunds and infinitives (*Jack's selling the bike was astonishing, For Jack to sell the bike would be astonishing*). But the gerund occurs in present and past tense contexts, not future contexts, while the infinitive occurs in hypothetical or future contexts. This fits with Bolinger's principle.

bother: this factive verb takes both gerunds and infinitives (*Laura's swimming across the lake at midnight bothered the counselors, For Laura to swim across the lake would bother the counselors*), but, as with *be astonishing,* the gerund is restricted to present and past contexts and the infinitive is restricted to hypothetical and future contexts, fitting with Bolinger's principle.

doubt: This nonfactive verb questionably takes gerunds, and infinitives not at all (*?Bo doubted Zack's finishing on time,* **Bo doubted for Zack to finish on time*). The uncertainty conveyed by *doubt* about the truth of the complement clause should, under Bolinger's principle, give rise to a preference for the infinitive over the gerund; so this verb is an exception or counterexample to Bolinger's principle.

be unfortunate: This factive adjective expression takes both gerunds and infinitives, like *be astonishing* and *bother,* with the same semantic distinction (*John's leaving early was unfortunate, For John to leave early would be unfortunate*).

Exercise 18:

remember: positive implicative. *John remembered to close the window* implies that John closed the window. But John's closing the window is not presupposed, so *remember* is not factive.

bother: factive. *It bothered us that George bounced the check* presupposes that George bounced the check.

neglect: negative implicative. *Max neglected to lock the door* implies that Max did not lock the door. But Max's not locking the door is not presupposed, so *neglect* is not factive.

avoid: negative implicative. *Leslie avoided answering the question* implies that Leslie did not answer the question. But Leslie's not answering the question is not presupposed, so *avoid* is not factive.

seem: neither. *John seemed to like Nancy* neither implies nor presupposes that John liked Nancy .

appreciate: factive. *The students appreciated the faculty senate's making linguistics a required course* presupposes that the faculty senate made linguistics a required course.

64

turn out: positive implicative: *It turned out that Jane married Mark* implies that Jane married Mark. But Jane's marrying Mark is not presupposed, so *turn out* is not factive.

suppose: neither. *Ed supposed that Frank would bring cookies* neither implies nor presupposes that Frank would bring cookies (only that Ed supposed that he would).

amuse: factive: *It amused the children that the spider could write in her web* presupposes that the spider could write in her web.

agree: neither: *Max agreed to sell Barb* the car neither presupposes nor implies that Max sold, or would sell, Barb the car. All the sentence implies (actually, entails) is what it literally says, that Max made an agreement to sell the car to Barb.

condescend: positive implicative: *Dick condescended to meet with the press* implies that Dick met with the press. But Dick's meeting withe the press is not presupposed, so *condescend* is not factive.

Exercise 19:

1. The dean asked [the students over for coffee]:

    conjunction: *The dean asked [the students over for coffee] and [the faculty members out for beer].* Passes.

    with expressions: *With the students over for coffee, the dean's children had to stay in their room.* Passes.

    Mad Magazine sentences: (The professor invited the students over for coffee.) *What? The students over for coffee! God forbid, we'll be charged with sexual harassment!* Passes.

    subject-only expressions: Fails. **The dean asked the cat out of the bag.*

    not + quantifier: *The dean asks not many students over for coffee, so be sure to go.* Passes.

    NP *alone: The dean asked the physics students alone over for coffee.* Passes.

    Conclusion: Small clause.

2. The coach wants [Max off the team].

    conjunction: *The coach wants [Max off the team] and [Joe on the starting five].* Passes.

    with expressions: *With Max off the team, the team will have much better chemistry.*

    Mad Magazine sentences: (The coach wants Max off the team.) *What? Max off the team? How will they ever defend against Doctor Dunkenstein?* Passes.

    subject-only expressions: Passes: *The coach wants the cat out of the bag.* (Situation: the coach wants to 'leak' some information.)

    not + quantifier: *The coach wants not many players off the team, just Max and Joe.* Passes.

NP *alone: The coach wants Max alone off the team.* Passes.

Conclusion: Small clause.

3. The referral service found [the family a good lawyer].

   conjunction: *The referral service found [the family a good lawyer] and [the company a good accountant].* Passes.

   with expressions: **With the family a good lawyer, the trial will be a breeze.* Fails.

   Mad Magazine expressions: (The referral service found the family a good lawyer.) **What? The family a good lawyer? They'll never be able to pay her!* Fails.

   subject-only expressions: Fails. While *The referral service found the cat out of the bag* is fine, it is not a paraphrase of **The referral found out of the bag for the cat.* But *The referral service found the family a good lawyer* can be paraphrased *The referral service found a good lawyer for the family.*

   not + quantifier: *?The referral service found not many families good lawyers.* Weak evidence; judgments differ.

   NP *alone: ?The referral service found our family alone a good lawyer.* Weak evidence; judgments differ.

   Conclusion: Probably not a small clause, though the evidence is not conclusive.

4. The judge found [Bugliosi a superb litigator].

   conjunction: *The judge found [Bugliosi a superb litigator] and [Jones a fine court reporter].* Passes.

   with expressions: *With Bugliosi a superb litigator, our side is bound to win.* Passes.

   Mad Magazine expressions: (The judge found Bugliosi a superb litigator.) *What? Bugliosi a superb litigator? I suppose he found Capone a great entrepreneur.* Passes.

   subject-only expressions: Passes: *The judge found the cat out of the bag.*

   not + quantifier: *The judge found not many lawyers superb litigators.* Passes.

   NP *alone: The judge found Bugliosi alone a superb litigator.* Passes.

   Conclusion: Small clause.

5. Please put [the car in the garage]:

   conjunction: *Please put [the car in the garage] and [the bike in the barn].* Passes.

   with expressions: *With the car in the garage, we are safe from intruders.* Passes. (However, this passing grade should be taken with a grain of salt. The acceptability of this example may stem from the fact that *the car in the garage* can be an NP with a head noun

66

and a modifying PP. Contrast *Please push the car into the river. What? ??The car ito the river? That's insane!*, which is worse.)

Mad Magazine expressions: (Please put the car in the garage.) *What? The car in the garage? Are you crazy? The garage is about to fall down!* Passes. (However, this passing grade should also be taken with a grain of salt, for the same reason as that discussed in connection with *with* expressions. Contrast *Please toss the ball into the basket. What? ??The ball into the basket? He'll never do it!*, which is worse.

subject-only expressions: Fails: **Please put the cat out of the bag.*

not + quantifier: **Hank puts not many cars in the garage.* Fails.

NP *alone:* **Please put the car alone in the garage.* Fails.

Conclusion: Probably not a small clause.

6. He lets [the cat out] before going to sleep.

conjunction: *He lets [the cat out] and [the dog in] before going to sleep.* Passes.

with expressions: *With the cat out, we knew the kitchen was likely to be scoured by marauding mice.* Passes.

Mad Magazine expressions: (He lets the cat out before going to sleep.) *What? The cat out? Does he want six litters of kittens in a year?* Passes.

subject-only expressions: *He lets the cat out of the bag whenever he is told a secret.* Passes.

not + quantifier: *He lets not many cats out.* (Unlikely situation; a better example might be *He lets not many cats in; this one is an exception.*) Passes.

NP *alone:* *He lets the cat alone out; the dog and the birds he keeps in.* Passes.

Conclusion: small clause.

Comment: As applied here, the conjunction test is useless to distinguish small clauses from other constructions. The reason is that these examples can be interpreted as cases of verb deletion: *The referral service found [the family a good lawyer] and FOUND [the company a good accountant] => The referral service found [the family a good lawyer] and ___ [the company a good accountant].* The conjunction might work better if the hypothesized small clauses were conjoined in contexts where no deletion analysis was possible, such as sentence-initially, but the contexts where small clauses are possible do not include such a position.

Additional exercise:

1. Two issues arise in determining the underlying structure of this sentence: what kind of structure *be sure* occurs in, and whether existential *there* is transformationally derived. The latter issue raises theoretical issues that are beyond the scope of this book; instead of addressing those issues, we shall follow classical transformational grammar and arbitrarily

assume that *there* is transformationally inserted, thus deriving a superficial structure containing *there* from an underlying structure that lacks *there*. The former issue is one we can straightforwardly address.

Since subject-only expressions (existential *there*, weather *it*, and subject chunks of idioms like can occur as subjects of *be sure*, as is the case with *seem, appear,* and the like, *be sure* can be assumed to have a structure like those expressions.

Consequently it makes sense to say that the underlying structure of this sentence is as follows: $[_S$ *A parade be on Sunday]* $[_{VP}$ *is sure]*. After "Raising" applies, which produces *A parade is sure to be on Sunday, there-* insertion applies, producing *There is sure to be a parade on Sunday.*

2. Since *apt* can take subject-only subjects (*It is apt be be raining, there is apt to be a big crowd there, The fur is apt to be flying if Marie raises that objection*), it patterns like *seem,* so the underlying structure may be assumed to be $[_S$ *It to be raining]* $[_{VP}$ *is apt]*.

3. What is the subject of the embedded verb *win*? A gap meaning 'Max.' *Try,* that is, is like *want.* So the underlying structure is *Max$_i$ tried* $[_S$ __$_i$ *to win Cathy's heart]*.

4. Underlying structure: *Cathy$_i$ condescended* $[_S$ __$_i$ *to come to the reception]*

5. Underlying structure: *Jon$_i$ was reluctant* $[_S$ __$_i$ *to go to State College]*.

6. Underlying and superficial structure identical: *Don imagined* $[_S$ *himself to be intelligent]*. *Himself* is the subject of the embedded clause rather than the direct object of the main clause because after *imagine* there can be subject-only expressions: *Don imagined it to be raining, Don imagined there to be a unicorn in the garden, Don imagined the cat to be out of the bag.*

7. Like the immediately preceding example.

8. *Continue* is like *seem,* because it can take subject-only expressions which must co-occur with expressions after *continue: The fur continued to fly, there continued to be problems, it continued to snow.* So the underlying structure is $[_S$ *Ollie to protest that he was innocent]* $[_{VP}$ *continued]*.

9. *My son a doctor* is a small clause. It passes the *with*, Mad Magaine, subject-only, *not* + Q, and NP *alone* tests: *With my son a doctor, I'll be sitting pretty in my old age,;What? My son a doctor? Never!; I intend to see the cat out of the bag; I intend to see not many of my sons doctors, but this one is special, I intend to see my son alone a doctor.*

Intend is a *want-* type verb.

Consequently the structure (underlying and superficial) is *I intend* $[_S$ __ *to see* $[_S$ *my son a doctor]]*.

Chapter Nine: Relative Clauses and Participles

Exercise 1:

1.   The coach was ⌈the one⌉ ⟨who⟩ seemed to be in charge.

2.   This is ⌈the cat⌉ ⟨that⟩ caught the rat.

3.   ⌈A car⌉ ⟨which⟩ you buy from a used-car lot can't be relied on.

4.   ⌈The instructors⌉ ⟨whom⟩ I complained to the dean about   are angry.

5.   Smith ordered ⌈the books⌉   about ⟨which⟩ Jones had boasted to him.

6.   ⌈The little boy⌉ came by ⟨who⟩ was trying to sell cookies.

Exercise 2:

1.   This is the cat that caught the rat.   (No gap; relative pronoun *that* functions as subject.)

2.   This is the man <u>whom</u> I met ___ yesterday.

3.   This is the cracked pipe <u>which</u> I told you about ___ on the plane.

4.   This is the leaky garage roof <u>about which</u> I was complaining ___.

5.   This is the class <u>to which</u> I was referring ___ in my report.

6.   The is the park ranger <u>whom</u> I wrote that awful letter to ___.

7.   The painting <u>that</u> Barbara did ___ of the market needs reframing.

8.   Cats who scratch furniture will be banned from the living room. (No gap; relative pronoun *who* functions as subject.)

Exercise 3:

1.

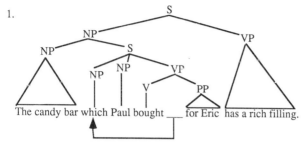

2.

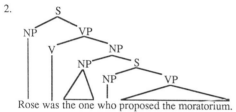

3.

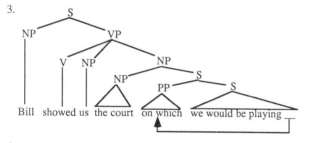

4.

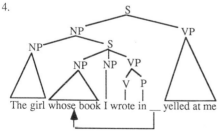

5.

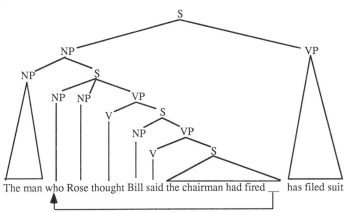

The man who Rose thought Bill said the chairman had fired ___ has filed suit

Exercise 4:

1. object of preposition.
2. direct object.
3. subject, subject, direct object.
4. sentence adverb.
5. object of preposition (and indirect object).
6. object of preposition.
7. subject.
8. sentence adverb.
9. sentence adverb.

Exercise 5:

1. relative clause: The proof that Bohr developed astonished the world of physics.
   that S: The proof that Nixon had ordered the coverup was available from early 1973.

2. relative clause: The possibility that you have suggested is frightening.
   that S: The possibility that cold fusion might be a reality astonished the world.

3. relative clause: The claim that the psychic made about the President seemed silly.
   that S: The claim that the President would resign in disgrace convinced no one.

4. relative clause: The hypothesis that William formulated was daring in its simplicity.
   that S: The hypothesis that there is a tenth planet in the solar system has many supporters.

5. relative clause: The notion that the committee came up with had possibilities for success.
   that S: The notion that election victories could be purchased like commodities bothered thoughtful commentators.

6.   relative clause: The dream that I had last night was scary.
      that S: The dream that our country could be free of racism inspired Martin Luther King.

Exercise 6:

1.   These examples suggest that *that* is a relative pronoun, not a complementizer.
      Complementizers can't take possessives, but relative pronouns can.

2.   Examples (a) - (d) have the opposite effect of the examples in (1), because they suggest that
      that is a complementizer. What follows each is a complete clause, with no gap, just what
      would be expected if *that* is a complementizer.
           But the last three examples undercut this evidence, because they contain instances
      of *who* behaving as a complementizer should, not a relative pronoun. These instances of
      who are followed by complete, gap-less, clauses, something that should not happen after a
      relative pronoun. These cases contain what are called 'resumptive' pronouns--
      ungrammatical gap-filling pronouns in relative clauses redundant because the relative
      pronouns and the extra pronouns bear the same grammatical relation. Examples like these
      are usually regarded as mistakes of 'performance,' not direct manifestations of
      'competence'--i.e., mistakes. If these are mistakes, there is no strong reason not to regard
      the examples of (2a-d) as mistakes too.

Exercise 7:

1.   restrictive relative clause: *Seven old ladies who got stuck in the lavatory complained to
      management.*
       nonrestrictive relative clause: *Seven old ladies, who were all wearing flowered dresses,
      arrived at the door of the pub.*

2.   restrictive relative clause: Impossible, because *Cathy and Max* has a specific referent that
      cannot be narrowed down, rather than constituting a restrictable set.

      nonrestrictive relative clause: *Cathy and Max, who had come over for dessert, announced
      that they were flying to Aruba on Saturday.*

3.   restrictive relative clause: *Anyone who comes in late should quietly take a seat at the back.*
      nonrestrictive relative clause: Impossible, because a nonrestrictive relative clause has to
      modify an NP with a unique referent, which *anyone* lacks.

4.   restrictive relative clause: *A box of crayons which Mama had bought for Ben was sitting
      on the corner of the table.*
      nonrestrictive relative clause: *A box of crayons, which Mama had bought for Ben, was
      sitting on the corner of the table.*

5.   restrictive relative clause: Hard to create because *my disk drive* appears to be specific, so it
      can't be narrowed down. But I may have two or more disk drives, so *My disk drive that
      crashed yesterday (not the one that is still working fine) will have to be taken to the shop* is
      possible.
      nonrestrictive relative clause: *My disk drive, which crashed yesterday, will have to be
      taken to the shop.*

6.   restrictive relative clause: *An alligator which seems to be sleeping may be quite alert.*

nonrestrictive relative clause: *An alligator, which seemed to be sleeping, lay inert on the mud as we quietly rowed past.*

7. restrictive relative clause: *Admnistration sources which refuse to indentify themselves can be a very useful, while frustrating, source of information to news gatherers.*
    nonrestrictive relative clause: *Administration sources, which refused to identify themselves, indicated that the invasion was still planned for some time within the next several hours.*

8. restrictive relative clause: Impossible, since this sentential expression is specific and can't be narrowed down to a subset. There is only one fact that Cathy took typing.
    nonrestrictive relative clausse: *The fact that Cathy took typing, which pleased the men in her family, didn't particularly impress her mother.*

Exercise 8:

1. Travelers who are staying at the conference center will be taken to the banquet by limousine.

2. Why don't you help those shoppers who are bagging their own groceries?

3. I want to own every record which is/was made by a Motown group.

4. Sue pointed out the man who was hidden in the crowd.

5. Most computers which are sold by discount stores can't be relied on.

6. Tim remembers every strikeout which was thrown by Steve Carlton.

Exercise 9:

1. not dangling.

2. dangling: *Having worked hard all morning.* Repair: e.g., *Having worked hard all morning, we now had the garage completely organized.*

3. dangling: *Studying intensely.* Repair: e.g., *Studying intensely, over a hundred students were in the cafeteria.*

4. not dangling.

5. dangling: *Pleased by Dana's progress.* Repair: e.g., *Pleased by Dana's progress, we figured that a B+ was the appropriate grade.*

6. dangling: *working round the clock seven days a week.* Repair: e.g., *Working round the clock seven days a week, Ellen finished her dissertation in six weeks.*

7. dangling: *assuming that we would win.* Repair: e.g., *The victory party was scheduled for Friday night on the assumption that we would win.*

Exercise 10:

Because sentence (b) contains an impossible progressive, impossible because the verb is instantaneous aspect and hence cannot occur in the progressive.

Exercise 11:

1. *The day dawning clear:* absolute.
2. *Barking madly:* non-absolute participle phrase.
3. *their fingers intertwined:* absolute.
4. *Born to a family of large landowners:* non-absolute participle phrase.
5. *The arena roof leaking:* absolute.
6. *fidgeting in his seat:* non-absolute participle phrase.
7. *Having failed twice:* non-absolute participle phrase.
8. *Unwilling to tackle Linguistics 1:* non-absolute participle phrase.
9. *Linguistics 1 being regarded as one of the most challenging courses in the catalog:* absolute.
10. *The coffee hot and the bagels ready:* absolute.

Additional exercises:

A.   Many possible answers.

B.   Nos. 1-4 contain participle expressions which cannot be related to relative clauses, since they are adverbial, modifying either the whole sentence or the VP. Consider just no. 1: **Bobby spent the night who was walking in the park* is ungrammatical, and its unextraposed variant *Bobby, who was walking in the park, spent the night* is not a paraphrase of the original. Nos. 2-4 are similar.

No. 5 contains a participle construction related to a relative clause.

No. 6 contains a participle construction which cannot be related to a relative clause since its verb, *have,* is stative, which cannot be progressive (as its ungrammatical relative clause source would have it: **Numbers which are having no factors other than one and themselves are prime*).

C.   Both the small clauses we looked at in Chapter Eight, and most absolutes, lack auxes. Absolutes may contain or omit verbs (*her fingers (being) numb*). Expressions like *her fingers numb* and *his socks still on the floor* can occur in both typical small clause positions (e.g., after verbs like *find* and *consider*) and in typical absolute positions (as sentence modifiers): *Mary found her fingers numb, Mary found his socks still on the floor; Her fingers numb, Mary could hardly work the buttons, His socks still on the floor, Jon smiled weakly at Mary.* Consequently, at least absolutes which lack auxes and verbs are small clauses. And some absolutes which contain verbs can occur in typical small clause positions too: *We found the day dawning clear, We heard the puppy barking, We saw the autumn leaves swirling around Lucien.*

But absolutes which contain auxes, and some which contain verbs, cannot occur in small clause positions: **The reporters considered the dissertation having been torn to pieces, *Fred's Publishing Co. found the dissertation being completely unpublishable.*

Exercise 1:

A.

1. The house that <u>she</u> is building will suit *Marian* very well.

The proexpression <u>she</u> can have *Marian* as its antecedent because although <u>she</u> precedes *Marian,* it doesn't c-command it. Under Rule 25 a proexpression is not allowed to bear "all possible" primary relations to its antecedent; the primary relations are "precedes" and "c-commands." The tree makes clear that <u>she</u> does not c-command *Marian,* since the first branching node dominating <u>she</u> is S, which does not dominate *Marian.*

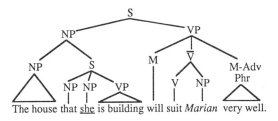

2. Ellen asked <u>them</u> whether *Irving and Lynette* could come for dinner.

The proexpression <u>them</u> cannot have *Irving and Lynette* as its antecedent, because <u>them</u> both precedes and c-commands *Irving and Lynette,* as can be seen from the tree:

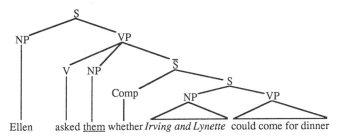

3. The fact that <u>he</u> studied preposing constructions made *Greg* a big success.

The proexpression <u>he</u> can have the NP *Greg* as its antecedent, because, while it precedes it, it does not c-command it:

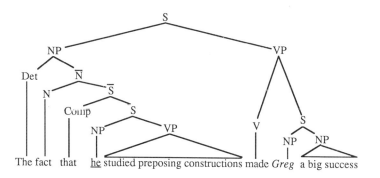

4.   We will award <u>it</u> to the one who wins *the prize*.

The proexpression <u>it</u> cannot use the NP *the prize* as its antecedent. It both precedes it and c-commands it:

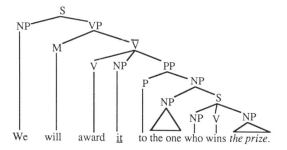

5.   It upset <u>them</u> that *Rose and Leon* had arrived before the others.

The proexpression <u>them</u> cannot use the NP *Rose and Leon* as its antecedent, because it both precedes and c-commands it:

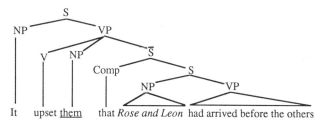

(Note that this analysis assumes that an extraposed clause is placed within the same VP--really, the same V-bar--as the antecedent. This is different from what was assumed in Chapter Six (p. 260).

6. The proexpression *he* can use the NP *John* as its antecedent since it follows it (and, for that matter, doesn't c-command it).

7. *He* left early, but *John* returned quite late.

The proexpression *he* cannot use the NP *John* as its antecedent, because *he* precedes *John*, the only possible primary relation in a conjoined structure.

B. In both, a pronoun and its putative antecedent cannot co-refer, despite the fact that the pronoun does not bear both primary relations to the putative antecedent. The pronouns may c-command their putative antecedents--if the sentences have structures like this--

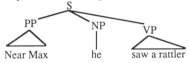

but do not precede them. (There is no guarantee the structure given above is right; another possible structure is the following--

```
                    S
              PP         S
           /    \      NP    VP
        Near Max       he  saw a rattler
```

If the latter structure is right, the pronoun *he* doesn't even c-command the putative antecedent *Max*.)

Exercise 2:

A. Because the reflexive pronoun *himself* does not have an antecedent appropriate in gender in the same minimal clause.

B. *Saul, Bill,* and *Max.* Only *Neil* cannot be an antecedent for *him.* The reason is that an ordinary pronoun canNOT have an antecedent within its minimal clause.

Exercise 3:

1. *The nominee$_i$ was delighted by the Senate's rapid confirmation of herself$_i$.

The minimal NP for the reflexive *herself* is [$_{NP}$ *the Senate's rapid confirmation of herself*]. Since that NP is within the minimal S containing the reflexive (the whole sentence), and the minimal NP contains another NP (*the Senate*), and there is no antecedent for *herself* within that NP, the sentence is bad.

2. The new Supreme Court justice$_i$ likes the biography of himself$_i$ written by a reporter for *USA TODAY*.

77

The minimal NP containing the reflexive is *[NP the biography of himself]*. But (see Rule 34's clause 2b) that NP does not contain another NP in addition to the reflexive. (The structure of that NP is *[NP the [Ñ biography of himself]]*.) So the reflexive requires an antecedent within its minimal S, not minimal NP; and one is there, *The new Supreme Court justice*. As a result the sentence is OK.

3.   I bought this new bike for myself.

There is no minimal NP containing the reflexive and another NP, so the antecedent for the reflexive must be within the minimal S, which in this case is the whole S. (The structure of the sentence is *[S I [VP bought [NP this new bike] [PP for [NP myself]]]]*.) There is an antecedent there, *I*. So the sentence is fine.

4.   *The picture I took of Steve₁ amused himself₁ .

This sentence is bad because it violates Rule 34's clause 3. There is no minimal NP containing an NP in addition to the reflexive, so the reflexive's antecedent must be within the minimal S. It is. But clause 3 requires that if the domain which must contain the antecedent is S, the antecedent must c-command the reflexive. It doesn't, as the tree shows:

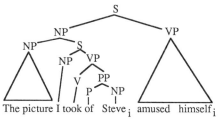

5.   *We're going to offer Sandra₁ a photo of her₁.

Rule 45 requires that an ordinary pronoun be "free" in its minimal Antecedent Category. It is, since the minimal NP or S is *a photo of her*. But it also requires (clause 3) that if the minimal AC contains no NP besides the pronoun (it doesn't, since the structure of that NP is *[NP a [Ñ photo [PP of her]]]*), the next-larger AC must not have a c-commanding antecedent. But it does, namely *Sandra*. Here is the tree for the sentence:

78

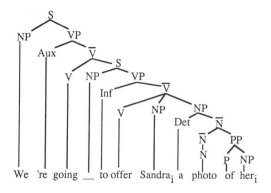

We 're going __ to offer Sandra_i a photo of her_i

6. Alice_i thought that Pete was going to invite her_i to the party.

    This sentence is fine. The ordinary pronoun *her* is free (does not have a c-commanding antecedent) within its minimal AC, the clause *Pete was going to invite her to the party.* Clause 3 of Rule 45 is not invoked because the minimal AC does contain an NP besides the pronoun (it has two, *Pete* and *the party.*)

7. Paul_i appreciated Jane's gift to him_i.

    The sentence is fine. Rule 45 requires that an ordinary pronoun be free within its minimal AC, which in this sentence is the NP *Jane's gift to him.* The pronoun *him* is free, because it has no c-commanding antecedent (*Jane* is the only NP besides *him* inside that NP, and *Jane* neither c-commands *him* nor matches it in gender).

Exercise 4:

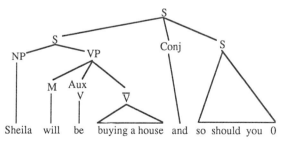

Sheila will be buying a house and so should you 0

The sentence is ambiguous between '...and so should you be buying a house' and '...and so should you buy a house.' In the former reading the antecedent of the 0 is *be buying a house,* which is not a constituent, and in the latter reading it is *buy a house,* which either is or is not a constituent depending on how the connection between *be* and *-ing* is treated. If *-ing* is part of a discontinuous morpheme *be...-ing,* it may not be part of the V̄, which would allow the antecedent to be a constituent. But if *-ing* is viewed as a morpheme unto itself, then *buy a house* is a part of the constituent *buying a house.*

Exercise 5:

1. Proexpression: *do it.* Antecedent: *write up the results.* (Calls for abstracting tense out of sentences.)

2. Proexpression: *so.* Antecedent: *The North Dakotans have invaded Montana.*

3. Proexpression: 0. Antecedent: *say that Sheila thought that Sam had moved out.*

4. No proexpression. (Note, however, that *got rid of her old man* is similar to a proexpression. It has the characteristic lowered stress of proexpressions, and is interpreted similarly to *divorced Fred* in the first clause.)

5. Proexpression: *do so.* Antecedent: *catch Willie in the stretch.* Tense must be abstracted out of both clauses; the proexpression does not include the tense. The reason is that any tense can occur in either clause: *L. attempted/will attempt/usually attempts to catch W. M will do so / usually does so.*

6. Proexpression: 0. Antecedent: *attempt to catch Willie in the stretch.*

7. Proexpression: 0. Antecedent: *attempt to catch Willie in the stretch.*

Exercise 6:

1. In B's utterance: *I did 0 too.* Antecedent: the $\bar{V}$ *think that that was the football.*

2. In B's utterance: *I did 0.* Antecedent: the $\bar{V}$ *take my red and blue striped tie.*

3. Because of the altered form of B's utterance, we cannot say exactly where the 0 is. Antecedent: no recognizable constituent, since B's utterance represents *Fred has not left yet* or *Fred has not yet left.*

4. At the end of the sentence. Antecedent: the $\bar{V}$ *bet (tenseless) on Precious Maiden.*

5. At the end of the sentence. Antecedent: the $\bar{V}$ *want to marry Zelda.*

6. No anaphoric 0; the proexpression is *do so.*

7. At the end. Antecedent: the $\bar{V}$ *marry Zelda.*

8. At the end of B's utterance. Antecedent: the VP *be going to be at the party.*

Exercise 7:

1.

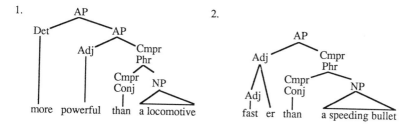

2.

3.

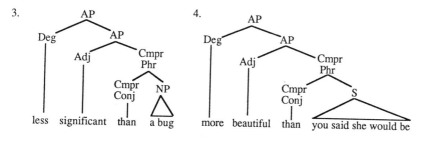

4.